UKRAINIAN EASTER EGGS

And How We Make Them

Library of Congress Catalog Card Number: 79-8477

ISBN 0-9602502-0-4

UKRAINIAN EASTER EGGS

And How We Make Them

by

Anne Kmit

Loretta L. Luciow

Johanna Luciow
and

Luba Perchyshyn

Ukrainian Gift Shop, 2422 Central Avenue N.E.
Minneapolis, Minnesota 55418

Dedicated to you,
the reader, in the hope
that your interest
in Ukrainian Easter eggs
will help continue
this beautiful
tradition.

Acknowledgments

When undertaking a project like a book, many people help to make it a success. We extend special thanks to Valia Poletz, who gave her time in the Ukrainian translations. Our thanks also go to Marie Procai, Elko Perchyshyn Jr., Becky Luciow, Very Reverend Michael Kudanovych, Robert Taylor, Mary Sicilia, Yaroslaw Elyiw, Irene Granovsky, Douglas Rivenburg, Elko Perchyshyn Sr., Nina Bulavitsky, Natalie Halstead, Helen Rychly, Iris Ivankevich, Dr. John Rosenow, Maureen Kadlec, Gabi Hemmersbach, Natalie Kmit, Rudy Gulstrand, Wasyl Ohar and Dennis Kmit.

We also wish to mention our photographer, Dave Kadlec, who made the sometimes tedious work of photography a pleasurable experience.

Table of contents

About the Authors

As a family, we have loved the art of making *pysanky* all our lives. We have taught the art to others, appeared on television and radio and have spent a great share of our time developing designs and techniques.

Johanna and her daughters, Loretta and Ann have co-authored three books concerning Ukrainian Art: *Eggs Beautiful*, 1975; a coloring book *Ukrainian Folk Designs to Color*, 1976; *Ukrainian Embroidery*, Van Nostrand Reinhold 1978. Theodore Luciow, Johanna's husband wrote many articles and books on Ukrainian history. The family continues in his literary footsteps.

Luba has developed an Easter egg kit which is sold throughout the United States and Canada. She, her sister Johanna, and their mother Marie Procai, have built an ethnic business, the Ukrainian Gift Shop of Minneapolis, which spreads the Ukrainian influence far and wide. Luba was featured in the recent award winning film, "Pysanka" by Slavko Nowytski in 1976. Besides making pysanky and embroidery, Luba paints Ukrainian ceramics.

This book is about the custom of decorating *pysanky* (Ukrainian Easter Eggs). We are so impressed with the wisdom and strength of our Ukrainian ancestors that we wanted to record a history of their tradition for others.

Through our studies, which involve five generations, we came to better understand our early ancestors, our grandparents our parents, and finally, ourselves and our children. From our work on this book, has come a greater love and appreciation of Ukrainian culture, history and tradition.

Luba Perchyshyn
Loretta L. Luciow

Johanna Luciow
Ann Kmit

Introduction

Ukraine is a nation of over fifty million people and a forgotten land in a real sense. The homeland of Ukraine reaches from the arc of the Carpathian Mountains down to the north shore of the Black Sea. It is bordered by Poland, Byelorussia, Russia and Rumania. The land is twice the size of Texas and is unusually rich and fertile. For centuries, it has been known as the "bread basket of Europe." Because it is rich in natural resources, such as oil, coal and iron, neighboring countries have struggled with Ukrainians for political and economic dominance. Today, Ukraine is one of the nations in the U.S.S.R., and although it has a seat in the United Nations, true freedom, which is prized in the United States, has eluded it.

Ukrainian immigration to the United States occured in two great waves. The first was before World War I, and the second was after World War II. Early in the twentieth century, American industry was expanding at a rapid rate. Manpower was solicited by American mining and foundry companies from Eastern European farming communities, in Ukraine, Poland and other countries.

OUR PERSONAL BEGINNINGS

It was during this first rush of Ukrainian immigration that Marie Sokol, our grandmother, came to America in 1912 as a young girl of fifteen. After living on a farm in Pennsylvania with her brother Paul for one-and-a-half years, she decided to travel to see her older brother in Winnipeg, Canada. In March of 1914, she set off with a few dollars and a small suitcase containing all her possessions. After a time, the train stopped in the Minneapolis Great Northern station for

This 1916 photo of Anthony (Tony) and Marie Procai shows them in Ukrainian costume as they appeared in one of the many play productions.

the evening. The next train to Winnipeg was scheduled to leave the following morning, so Marie decided to find a place to stay for the night. In her limited English, she asked a policeman if there were any Ukrainians living in the city. He directed her to 2nd street south, several blocks from the station, close to the frozen Mississippi River. It was completely dark when she found the street. There were only five houses there, all quiet and closed against the cold night. It seemed as if the third house was the right one! She knocked. When the door opened, she asked in Ukrainian, "Are you Ukrainian?". A man and woman answered a surprised "yes" and invited her into their home. They told Marie of a young Ukrainian woman staying with them named Katheryn Dacko. "She is my cousin!", Marie said in surprise. Because it was late, Katheryn was already asleep. The couple led Marie to her cousin's room where she gently shook Katheryn's shoulder. She opened her eyes sleepily and said, "Is it you, Marie?" They joyfully hugged each other, crying and laughing at the same time.

Marie decided that she would stay in Minneapolis and was refunded the rest of her ticket to Canada. She must stay in Minneapolis; was it not God's will that led her to her only family in the state?

Even though she spoke almost no English, she found work as a waitress! She earned her living as she learned to speak English. She learned how to survive in America. She found a place to live and joined with a group of young Ukrainians in a church choir.

During the fifteen year period between 1915 and 1930, years before movies or radio, young people banded together in ethnic groups and put on plays and programs for entertainment and fun. Marie was a natural actress, and she preformed in starring roles 87 times. The young troup toured Minnesota and Wisconsin, going to Superior, Duluth and St. Paul to put on plays. The money which they raised went to help build their new church in Northeast Minneapolis. The stories Marie tells us of this period in her life speak of courage and excitement.

During this period Marie met Tony Procai, a handsome Ukrainian immigrant, who had come to the United States with his two brothers, shortly before Marie's arrival, and had settled in Minneapolis. Tony sang in the church choir and acted in the plays of the young Ukrainian amateur group. He and Marie worked to retain their heritage in America. They married in 1915 and settled down and eventually they raised four children.

Marie Procai shows part of a family collection of art and historical artifacts which are on permanent display in the Minneapolis Gift Shop.

As Marie established her own home, she remembered that as a little girl in Western Ukraine, she had watched her grandmother wax and dip colored eggs with the traditional designs for Easter. When she was five years old, she was taken by her parents to live in Slavonia, now a part of Yugoslavia, where only a few old-time crafts were carried on. In Minneapolis, she became homesick and tried decorating eggs again.

She had no tools or dyes, but that did not stop her. She fashioned a *kistka* (writing tool) from the metal tip of a shoe lace. She bought crepe paper and made dyes by soaking the paper in boiling water and allowing it to cool.

After she had asked God's blessing, she slowly applied the hot bees wax to a fresh hen's egg. She made the basic first lines. Then she dipped an egg into the home made colors and gradually added wax to her design. Her first egg was simple, but when she held it in her hand, it seemed to come from her early years in Ukraine.

14

Tony enjoyed working with ceramics. He made his own molds and poured the clays before he painted the Ukrainian designs.

Here in America, where another language and another culture were becoming part of her life, she managed to hold onto her roots!

As her young family grew, she continued to perform in church plays, and each year before Easter, she made *pysanky* (decorated Easter eggs). Women's clubs, girl scout troups and other organizations called upon her to demonstrate the art and set up displays. In her own way, she educated many people in Ukrainian traditions.

Tony Procai tended a huge garden and worked as a baker all his life. When he retired, he began to make and paint ceramics, and his late blooming talent was a source of joy. His ceramic work followed traditional Ukrainian patterns and had he lived longer, his talents would have reached many more people. He won many ribbons from the Minnesota State Fair.

Marie and Tony Procai, with their love of traditional art, have added thousands of designs which will delight and inspire generations to come.

CHAPTER 1

Traditional Background

PRE-CHRISTIAN

$\mathbf{P}$rimitive man lived in a world of unexplained wonders. In an attempt to find reasons for heavenly and earthly mysteries, ancient people universally worshipped the sun. It was the sun which warmed the earth and was the source of all life. In the area which is now Ukraine, eggs were chosen for sun worship ceremonies, for when an egg was broken, the yolk represented the sun and the whites, the moon. Eggs were deeply important in spring rituals of these primeval men. During the winter, the earth was dormant and appeared to be without life, just as an egg appeared to be void of life. But when spring came, new life came forth; the egg was a perfect symbol of the sudden burst of life from dormancy.

References to *pysanky* can be found in developing Ukrainian poetry, art, songs and all facets of life where the decorated egg was represented as a benevolent talisman. People of all ages believed the eggs had power to help them in their daily lives.

Ancient *pysanky** were not the product of single artists or even of single villages but were representative of the whole nation. The designs, the colors, the legends, and the craftmanship of *pysanky* developed as Ukrainian culture became more complex. Today's *pysanky* are an echo of the past.

Then as now, each person had needs for peace, beauty and creativity, and, to the women of the past, making *pysanky* was a harmonious and satisfying experience. At the same time, they believed the eggs possessed special powers.

They gave *pysanky* as a sign of good wishes and fortune telling. Children received light colorful *pysanky* with floral designs. Teenagers received eggs decorated with a great deal of white,

*Plural of pysanka. The plural of many Ukrainian words is formed in this way.

signifying that their future was a blank page which was yet to be written. The *hospodari* (married couples) received 40 triangle eggs. They were working with their families and farms and appreciated the power in all facets of their lives which the 40 triangle egg represented (see page 37, egg 11). The old received black eggs with belts, ladders and gates, which represented heavenly bridges. The same kind of eggs were carried to the cemeteries of the ancestors. White eggs with simple designs were usually reserved for the graves of little children.

Pysanka designs as a national ornament evolved continually as all art forms do. Because people and times are always changing, new symbols appeared and old ones faded away. Meanings of the symbols gradually changed as well. Perhaps this explains the multitudes of *pysanka* symbols. One fact is certain: There is no life without art, and the *pysanka* is a folk art which has been the pulse of the Ukrainian nation.

Following are some of the traditions and legends which were part of every village in Ukraine. Some of the stories make us smile in todays technical world, but others cause us to stop and note the true and deep respect which the simple folk had for nature. Natural symbols were central to the *pysanky* created by Pre-Christian people.

PRE-CHRISTIAN STORIES AND TALES

TREES

According to an old Ukrainian belief, when a wounded tree cried, it shed tears like a person. It also bled when it was hurt, and the bark protects it just as the skin protects a person. The ancient Ukrainians were convinced that a tree had a soul and should be honored as one honors a friend.

This belief was practical, especially in reference to fruit trees. For example, a popular story is told about a man who dared to cut down a pear tree so he could build his house on that spot. He immediately experienced painful misfortunes. His horse died, the cow gave bad milk, and his wife began to nag as she never had before. One day, in his misery, he noticed the tough roots of the pear tree sending up shoots through the floor boards of his house. He knew he was beaten, he took down his house and planted seven young fruit trees (seven was a mystical number).

His wife became good natured and loving, his cow gave good milk once again and he was able to buy a finer horse than the one he had before! He was relieved of his punishment because the soul of the old pear tree now lived in the seven fruit trees and was at peace.

Another tale tells of a man and wife who had a beautiful apple orchard. In this orchard, however, there was one tree which bore very little fruit. To solve the problem, the couple went into the orchard where the wife stood behind the tree. The man raised an ax and said three times in a strong voice, "Will you bear fruit or not?" Each time, the wife said, as if speaking for the tree, "Yes, I will." The man then tied a rope around the trunk of the tree to seal the promise, and the next year it bore fruit! This is how to make a tree obey, so the story goes.

Blown eggs were used to decorate fruit trees in the spring. In the hopes of plentiful harvest of fruit, the farmers would hang eggs in the orchards and in the young trees surrounding the house. Not only did it assist the fruiting, but it was a beautiful sight to behold.

In another tradition, a young tree was carefully dug up from the land of the groom and replanted near the home of the bride-to-be. The ritual was customarily performed in May, and it provided a symbolic, living tie between the two merging households.

SPIDERS AND WEBS The spot where a spider web was found was considered to be a lucky place. If there were webs in the barn, the farmer felt that the productivity of the cows would be assured. If a person removed a web from the barn, it was feared that the quality of the cream would diminish or even disappear. "If there is no web, there is no cream" is an old Ukrainian saying.

In those days, if a person was looking for a place to build a house, he would set a pot containing a small amount of cream on the proposed site. A spider was quickly placed in the pot and then it was covered. A few days later, it was opened. If the spider had begun to spin a web over the cream, the site was a lucky one for a new home.

For weather forcasting, farmers noted the web building habits of the spiders in the fields. If the webs were lightly built, the farmers expected a long spell of calm warm weather.

When needed for medicinal reasons, a spider could be killed but only with the back of the hand. The custom was to kill a spider and wipe the hand on the forehead of a sick animal. The power of the spider would make the animal well, so they said. In cases of bleeding on the hand or foot, it was very common to wrap a web around the wound to stop the bleeding.

A beautiful legend comes to us concerning the origin of *pysanky*. The story says that the first *pysanky* came from the sky.

A cold and bitter winter had swept across the land with such speed that the migrating birds had no chance to fly to warmer lands. They suffered greatly in the chilling cold and began to fall to the ground, too cold to fly or take care of themselves.

The peasants gathered the frozen creatures and brought them into their homes. There, the birds were fed and warmed throughout the harsh winter. When spring arrived, the peasants opened their homes and allowed the birds their freedom.

The birds flew away for several days and when they returned, they brought back a decorated *pysanka* for each of the peasants in thanks for saving their lives. Ever since that time, according to the story, *pysanky* were decorated in the spring.

Each segment of society used *pysanky* in different ways developing its own traditions and stories concerning the power of the egg.

BIRDS

In the spring, farmers would take a decorated egg and stroke it on the chests of the oxen and other beasts of burden so that the harnesses would not rub them. The farmer would then bury the egg in the soil of his field to insure a large, bountiful harvest.

Blown eggs were hung on a string above the barn door because the farmers believed that the barn would then be safe from fire and lightning. Before a stranger could enter the barn, he was asked to look at the blown egg to protect the animals from the "evil eye". The most important primative symbol was the circle. Farmers made circles over the doors of the barns with white-wash, charcoal or chalk to protect all who passed within, human or animal.

If caught in a storm, a farmer would clear a circular patch of ground and place sticks at the edge, and then stand in the circle. "Step inside the circle of protection", he would say, believing in its magical strength. Once he was inside, he felt no harm would come to him. It is no surprise that the circle was the most used symbol on the *pysanka*.

FARMERS

Spring in Ukraine does not come without a struggle! When the first vegetation filled the fields with little yellow flowers, the shepherds gathered them and wove *vinky* (garlands of flowers worn around the head by maidens in Ukraine) to place on the heads of all the animals with horns. What a beautiful sight when the sheep, goats and cattle were herded into the villages wearing golden crowns of flowers. It was an early sign of spring.

SHEPHERDS

Shepherds also used circle symbols. After Christianity was introduced, it was the old shepherds who were most afraid of vampires since they were separated from the village by many miles. They believed that newly dead souls might rise and drink the blood of the living in the darkest hours before dawn.

To neutralize this evil power, an old shepherd would go to the cemetary in the early evening and draw a circle around himself near the grave of the newly deceased. There, he would sit with a clay figure balanced on his head. The figure represented the priest who had blessed the previous crops. He waited in a quiet vigil throughout the night, and the circle of protection kept him safe from evil. When the sun began to rise, he knew that the power of the vampire had been "worked away". Shepherds of old Ukraine must have been very brave!

MAIDENS

In May, during the evening of the holiday "Ivana Kupala", maidens gathered by a fast flowing river or stream. Each girl would release a delicate *vinok* in the stream. Wherever the *vinok* landed would be the place from which her lover would come. If it floated to the opposite shore, she knew he would come from that direction. If the *vinok* sank in the stream, the girl must be careful that she didn't become an old maid. If the *vinok* came apart, nothing would come of her hopes for the young man on her mind and she must wait until another time.

A shortage of water during a drought was handled by Ukrainian peasants in the following manner. A girl around the age of 14 was sent to another source of water, a well or a stream, several miles away. She would take a mouthfull of water and bring it back home and spit it into the dry stream or river bed. Only then could the people expect the mircale of rain. They fully believed nature would fill its part of the bargain.

Ukrainian Easter

The background of the *pysanka* is an echo of an ancient people who respected nature. A people who worked hard to survive, the Ukrainians used the *pysanka* in mystical and magical rites which were considered necessary for their survival. As we have seen, decorated eggs were intimately related to the greeting of spring. A beloved and blessed object, the decorated egg represented the happy holiday where life won out over death, spring over winter. The symbolism of the *pysanka* has brought hope, happiness, and protection from evil to the Ukrainians for many centuries before the introduction of Christianity.

With the advent of Christianity new meanings were added to old symbols, but many of the old symbols survived as well. Because the meanings and significance were so important to the peasant people, early missionaries incorporated the *pysanka* into Christian belief and used it to bring more people to Christ. Although a great deal has been forgotten, it is clear that the *pysanka* was a gentle creation which helped pre-Christian and Christian Ukrainians to deal with everyday problems of life, love and death.

Pysanky tell so much about vanishing attitudes toward nature and life. For example, in the 19th century and the beginning of the 20th century, *pysanky* were included in the grave with a child if he died during the Easter holiday season. The grieving family believed the child would have something to play with as well as something to eat if he got hungry. In the case of the death of a maiden, since she never had a chance to fall in love and give a *pysanka* to a young man, beautiful *pysanky* were gently placed around her head in the form of a wedding *vinok*. Only the finest eggs were used for this purpose and she was buried with the mystical promise of a wedding. Belief in an after-life was a strong part of the Ukrainian philosophy of death. Both of these illustrations provide us with examples of the intermingling of pagan and Christian beliefs.

In pre-Christian times, the *pysanky* were created only during the spring festivities revolving around worship of the sun.

The most important holiday on the church calendar in Ukraine is Easter, which is also a spring celebration. Traditionally, Easter is much more than a three day period. It begins with the first day of Lent and lasts a full 40 days.

After church on Ash Wednesday, life became very different from the normal routine. Eggs, meats and dairy products were no longer eaten on fast days (Monday, Wednesday and Friday). Different foods were served using oil, bread, noodles and simple vegetables such as cabbage. The family reverently gave up a rich portion of their diet as a form of physical purification in preparation for the great day.

Next during the Lenten season, the house was completely and vigorously cleaned. Feather beds were aired, rugs were beaten, the kitchen was whitewashed from top to bottom, and every corner was scrubbed and polished. In a real sense, the home was purified for Easter, too.

Last and most importantly, the process of mental purification began. If there had been arguments with the neighbors or relatives during the past year, this was the time to make ammends. Anger and bad feelings were neutralized with forgiveness.

The fasting, house cleaning and active settlement of problems in a 40 day period was an age-old psychological strengthener for the spirit of the Ukrainian peasant. It truly readied him for Easter and spring and enriched his life.

If possible, new clothes were made for every member of the family. Rooted in ancient tradition in the spring rites, when primitive man realized that nature was changing its dreary winter colors for spring splendor, it became the custom to brighten one's personal wardrobe as well. Now with Eastertide, at least one article of clothing was bought or made for each member of the family in honor of the Resurrection. If someone was very poor, he would buy only shoelaces, but he would have something new no matter what.

HOLY WEEK OBSERVANCE

During the last week of the Lenten season, the churches filled with worshippers. On Thursday of Holy Week, called *Strastney Chetver*, signifying the day of suffering, the priest read the Bible in twelve intervals describing the suffering of Christ while carrying the cross. At each interval, the members of the congregation bowed and touched their foreheads to the floor three times *(poklony)*. There were no pews in the church. It was a matter of fact that after years of this reverent service, many church floors were uneven and worn from the foreheads touching the floor over and over.

On Good Friday, a large painting of the dead Christ *(Plaschivnytsia)* was displayed in front of the altar with candles burning around it. Regular church lamps were dimmed, and in the semi-darkness, the church members mourned before the "Tomb of Christ".

EGG DECORATING RITUAL

Before a Ukrainian woman could make *pysanky*, she was supposed to be in a perfect spiritual state of mind. The previous day was spent peacefully: She would avoid gossip, deal with her family patiently and cook a good dinner.

Pysanky were made at night after the children were asleep. Only women in the family could work together and no one else was allowed to peek, since the purpose of creating *pysanky* was to transfer goodness from the household to the designs and push away evil. This was a mystical expression and not a social event. The fresh eggs were gathered from hens where a rooster was in residence, for, according to belief, if *pysanky* were made on non-fertile eggs, there would be no fertility in the home.

The women in the family asked different blessings for each egg, for they felt their good wishes traveled with the *pysanka*. Special songs were sung quietly, so the souls *(dukhe)* which were said to inhabit the night, would not be disturbed.

Small clay pots were used to hold the dyes which had been made using secret family formulas. The wax lines were drawn on the eggs, and slowly, the simple shells became filled with ancient symbolism, color and harmony.

Even now, looking at *pysanky*, one is struck by the inner rules in the placement of the motifs. The composition may seem free and random, but actually it is done according to rythmical placing of color and proportion. The division of spaces is also important, and each artist cares about the graphic placement of elements, intuitively understanding the unwritten rules. Technical talent developes in all artists, although only a few reach the highest level. But it is not the most important consideration, for the rythym, balance, color and creativity are more significant. The most important quality of the *pysanka*, however, is the power and love which the egg conveys, and all of Ukraine was aware of this.

The process took several evenings to finish. In a large family, 60 eggs would be completed by Holy Thursday.

The finished eggs would be placed in a very large bowl in the oven. As the oven warmed the eggs, each one was taken out and the melted wax was wiped off carefully with a clean cloth. This cloth was not thrown away: later, it was burned in the oven when the *pasky* (Easter bread) were baked for the Easter feast to come.

Here is a partial list of how the *pysanky* would be used:

1. *One or two were given to the priest.*
2. *Three or four were taken to the cemetery and placed on graves of the family.*
3. *Ten to fifteen were given to small children and God-children.*
4. *Ten to twelve were exchanged by the unmarried girls with the eligible young men in the community.*
5. *Several were saved to place in the coffin of loved ones who might die during the coming year.*
6. *Several were saved to keep in the home for protection from fire and storms.*
7. *Two or three were placed in the trough where the animals ate, so they would have many young.*

8. *At least one egg was placed beneath the bee hive to insure a good harvest of honey.*

9. *One was saved for each grazing animal to be taken out to the fields with the shepherds in the spring.*

Everyone from the oldest to the youngest received a *pysanka* for Easter.

Krashanky were also made at this time. They are hard-boiled, solid-colored eggs which were originally dyed red. With time, *krashanky* were dyed with many other colors too (except for black). They were important in the Easter holiday for they were the first food which would be eaten to break the fast after the long Lent. Also, Easter games were played with these edible eggs.

Shells of *krashanky* were thrown in the rows of the garden to bless the harvest. To be sure the chickens would hatch many chicks, *krashanky* shells were placed in the nests of the chickens in the hen houses. Also, for good luck, *krashanka* shells were thrown in fast running streams. Young girls washed their faces in water which had red shells soaking in it. They believed it would make them more beautiful, and, indeed, the red color brought a blush to their cheeks.

PREPARATION OF THE EASTER FOODS AND THE EASTER BASKET

The Easter foods were prepared during the last few days of Lent. Imagine, for a moment, how wonderful the rich yeast breads smelled as they baked. Each *paska* (Easter bread) contained as many as twelve egg yolks and one cup of melted butter. The loaves were carefully baked in tall cylindrical pans so that when they were eased from the pans, they resembled tall brown mushrooms. The aroma was doubly tempting because they could not be eaten until after the blessing of the food baskets on Easter morning.

Another aroma permiated the air from the smokehouse. Hams, bacon and sausages hung in readiness. Like the bread, they smelled even better because they couldn't be eaten until later.

Next, horseradish was ground to a fine mash. Cooked beets were grated with a little honey and vinegar and mixed with the root. This bitter food was eaten at Easter to remind everyone of the harsh trials which were endured by Christ at the time of His crucifixion.

On Easter eve, a basket was prepared containing a number of symbolic foods. The basket was lined with a clean embroidered cloth. Next came the large round *paska*, horseradish, a few *krashanky*, sausage and perhaps ham or bacon, salt, cheese, one or two decorated *pysanky* and butter. Often, the butter was shaped in the form of a lamb. A small red flag was placed with the lamb to show that

Christ is the Lamb of God and through His death, death was conquered for all. Later, the butter lamb would be placed at the center of the table.

The basket was then covered with another beautiful embroidered cloth. The entire family would dress carefully in their best clothing and carry the basket to church. The Mass began shortly before midnight and lasted until about 2:30 in the morning. Twelve o'clock midnight was the first time the priest proclaimed "Khrystos Voskres", (Christ is risen!). The congregation answered with, "Voisteno Voskres!" (He is risen, indeed!). The church choir sang many chants with these words as well.

When the great Mass had ended about 2:30 a.m., the baskets were placed outside around the church building in a circle. A candle was thrust in each *paska* and lit so that there was a flickering circle all around in the darkness. The parishoners stood back, and the priest and the altar boys made a joyous procession as the priest sprinkled holy water and blessed the baskets. Everyone was tired but happy, and it was time to go home.

EASTER SUNDAY

Eggs were exchanged on this day: Bright designed eggs among the young, darker deeper *pysanky* among the old. Everywhere, you heard the greeting "Khrystos Voskres" and the answering reply, "Voisteno Voskres". Kisses, good wishes, *pysanky* and love were all a part of the day. The baskets which had been blessed were unpacked, and the table was set for the feast of Easter. The long disciplined period of self-denial was over; spring had begun, and life began again with new energy.

After eating the blessed food, the families went to the cemeteries surrounding the churches. The young girls danced *"hayivky"*, Easter dances which represent the meandering movement of the sun and the moon. Young boys played games with *krashanky*, and all the activity was believed to be shared by the departed souls who rested in the graves. Families broke *krashanky* and sprinkled the hard-cooked egg and shells over the grave of their loved ones, saying "Khrystos Voskres". Much later, when everyone had gone home, it was believed that the birds who came to eat the food scattered there, were really the souls of their dear departed ones.

EGG GAMES WITH "KRASHANKY"

Many games were played by the boys in the grassy cemetery on Easter Sunday. *"Karbuliuliu"* was played by boys from 4 to 6 years of age. They sat on the grass in a square formation. Each boy had a *krashanka*, and on signal, it was rolled diagonally to the opposite corner. In the activity, some of the eggs became cracked. The boy with the cracked egg was out, and another boy with a fresh *krashanka* came in to take his place. The last boy to remain with an unbroken egg was the winner.

Another variation of *"Karbuliuliu"* was played by the older boys, up to the age of 16. They chose rounded *krashanky* and threw the eggs high up into the air, hoping the egg would land in the soft grass without cracking. Those whose eggs landed safely in the first round continued in the next round of throws. Each time, there were fewer boys and *krashanky* until there was only one boy left. He was the winner in the throwing contest.

The game, *"Kranakohuta"* required three boys. One stood in the center and was the "rooster" *(Kohut)*. Those on the ends threw a *krashanka* to each other, trying not to let the *"kohut"* catch it and also try not to let the egg break. When the boy in the middle succeeded in catching the egg, he changed places with the boy who made the last throw, and there was a new *"kohut"*. The game required considerable skill and was great fun for all.

Cooked *Krashanky* were tapped together in another game, *"Chockania krashankamy"*. Only one egg would break when two eggs were tapped so the winner took his opponents cracked egg and looked for more conquests. Boys also rolled eggs into each other, hoping their opponents egg would crack so they could gather the winnings and collect the most eggs.

"KOLODA"

In pre-Christian and Christian times, the god of love and marriage, *Koloda*, was honored in a complicated fashion. According to *Koloda*, young men and women who were not married by spring had to pay a ransom. During the first week of Lent, married women of the village banded together in a light hearted spirit and went from house to house to find all the unmarried young people. When they found someone, after a mock struggle, they would tie a small log on the left

Girls give the prettiest eggs to boys on Easter Sunday.
Elko Perchyshyn Jr. receives a pysanka from Becky Luciow.

arm of the young person to show that a debt must be paid to *Koloda*. In the spirit of fun, the parents of the young person would say sternly, "You deserve to drag this log around: you did not get married when I told you to!" The log would be worn until after the Easter feast.

To break the debt which the log signified, a girl had to give a *pysanka* to a young man at Easter. Often, she gave him a beautifully embroidered scarf as well. If she wished, she could be fickle and give several eggs to several young men for she was not limited to one single suitor. As for the young man, he had to "rent music" or pay for a dance for each girl who had given him a *pysanka*. Thus, his log could be removed and he was free from his debt to *Koloda*.

More recently, the log worn by the girls has been beautifully decorated with ribbons and bows. This was a "womans' holiday", so said the amused men, which honored love and marriage. It was celebrated throughout Ukraine with many local variations.

CHAPTER 2

Traditional Symbols

Symbolism of Color on "Pysanky"

The most ancient *pysanky* were made very simply with only two colors. Gradually, as the peasant folk became intimate with nature and learned to create other colors, more variety was used to decorate the eggs. All of the colors had symbolic significance although they did not always mean the same thing.

Dyes were usually prepared by boiling a substance in water until desired color was obtained. Vinegar was often added to strengthen the color. The procedures used to make the dyes were a family secret, passed down to female family members of succeeding generations.

WHITE White is the color of most chicken eggs, and, therefore, no white dye was needed. It is rare to see a *pysanka* which does not use a great deal of the white color. White symbolizes purity. Sometimes, after an egg was decorated in several colors, it was gently bleached with sauerkraut juice so that the background color was white. Eggs with totally white backgrounds were usually reserved for the graves of younger children.

YELLOW Yellow dye was made from dry onion skin, bark of the wild apple tree, buckwheat husks and the flower of the lilac. The color on *pysanky* meant the moon and the stars and generally symbolized a successful harvest and wisdom.

GREEN Green meant spring, rebirth of nature and the wealth of the plant kingdom. "Green is pleasant all over the world", is an old Ukrainian saying. The color also represented freshness, untouched happiness and youth and was an age old symbol of innocence. The color was made from winter rye, wheat, various grasses and leaves such as myrtle.

Blue meant sky, air, magic, and good health. Blue was used in small amounts to add contrast to warm colors and is considered to be an active color. The dye was prepared from marrow or logwood.

BLUE

The orange color represents power endurance and ambition. Passion is red, wisdom is yellow and the combination of these two colors gives us the sun colors of orange and everlasting warmth.

ORANGE

Red is the most vigorous color and means the sun, happiness in life, hope, and passion. Even though it is the color of spilled blood, it connotes nobility, bravery and enthusiasm. Red is the most favorite of all colors among Ukrainian artisans. Dyes were made from red onion skins, raspberries, rose-hips, beet juice or old fashioned plums. In the 19th century, red dye was made from imported brazilwood.

RED

The color brown was a positive symbol representing the color of the earth and the color of the far away mountains. It was also tied in with the harvest since it is a color of fall. The dye was made from oak bark, tea or coffee.

BROWN

Grey is a dillution of black and is not usually a positive color. Grey is sometimes used to separate two chromatic colors such as red and green. Grey dye was made by diluting charcoal in water to the desired shade.

GREY

The color of the highest vibration, purple was always associated with royalty. On *pysanky*, it represents faith and trust.

PURPLE

Black often signified the darkest time before dawn. In Ukrainian tradition, the period between the first and third crow of the rooster, was a time when souls of the dead (*dukhe*) were thought to travel. This was the "blackest time of the night". Black dye was made from oak bark or from walnut husks. The simplest way to make black dye, however, was to collect soot from the fireplace and mix it with hot water.

BLACK

The color combination of black and white represented protection from evil. Eggs decorated with black and white designs were also made to honor departed souls. These eggs, generally decorated with bridges and gates were given to older people.

BLACK AND WHITE

COMBINATIONS OF COLORS

Using several colors together meant various things to the artist. Each region had its typical color blends so it is difficult to catagorize the combinations. However, we do know that color combinations denote more power than solid colored eggs. For example, a woman must create a four colored egg to neutralize a bad family separation.

Story Eggs

After searching through old Ukrainian books and talking to several wise egg makers, we have gathered 27 "story eggs". These eggs, pictured on pages 36, 37 and 44 are each accompanied by a short descriptive paragraph which gives a glimpse into the past and reflects the strong belief in nature which was so much a part of the Easter egg tradition.

Symbolism of nature on "Pysanky"

The most ancient and widely used symbol is the sun. Graphically presented in unlimited designs, the sun appears as a circle, a flower or a spiral. We find it calm, moving and at other times, it just sends rays. The source of light and life, the sun originally had magical meanings and was considered a god in pre-Christian times. Gradually, the solar symbol lost its magical interpretation and became a most beloved ornament used in *pysanky* and embroidery designs.

SUN

Ever since ancient times, the star symbol represented success. Stars are represented with even numbers, six or eight points, because they are much easier to draw and also because even numbers were believed to foretell good fortune.

    The star is one of the most popular symbols used on *pysanky* and is second in importance only to the sun.

STAR

Birds are delicate symbols which represent spring, good harvests, and the "pushing away" of evil. Often, only a part of the bird is included in the design: beak, eye, cone, feet, wing or head. Partial bird designs carried the same meaning as the whole bird.

BIRDS

As in many cultures, the heart is the symbol of love in Ukrainian folklore. The heart is generally the center of the motif in *pysanka* designs and all other patterns supported the main composition.

HEART

Fruits and vegetables meant more than a good harvest. They meant a good life. The designs were used symbolically to beckon all plant life to grow and ripen more quickly. Common symbols are peas, cherries and apples. The *pysanka* pictured on page 36 represents growing cucumbers.

FRUITS AND VEGETABLES

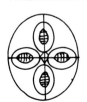

FLOWERS

The many colorful flowers on *pysanky* freely represent beauty and children. Sometimes it is hard to separate the flower designs from the sun designs since they can be depicted in a similar manner, but flower designs have little mystical significance and are represented for their beauty alone.

WHEAT

For many centuries, the symbol of wheat has signified the life's work of the Ukrainian peasant. Sheaves of wheat are usually a small part of the *pysanky* design in a larger central motif.

SPIDERS

The motif of the spider is an ancient one which is credited with healing powers and good fortune. Grandparents warned children not to kill spiders, for there was an old saying, "Having a spider in the house brings Good Luck." According to Ukrainian tradition, spiders spun webs to cover the trail of the Holy Family on their flight to Egypt.

Paska is the traditional Easter bread which is made with many eggs and pure butter. The Easter table is often set with the paska in the center, surrounded by decorated pysanky.

Very Reverend Michael Kudanovych of St. Michaels Ukrainian Orthodox Church in Minneapolis, blesses the baskets of Easter foods. Paritioners of all ages partake in this service.

ANIMALS

Prosperity and wealth are symbolized by animals. *Pysanky* with these designs were also believed to have a positive effect on farm animals and their good health. Common animals used are horses, cows, lambs, deer, and rams.

LADDERS

Ladders were incorporated on *pysanky* intended primarily for older people, since they would soon be entering another existence. The ladder signified a higher level representing the ascent to heaven. Generally, eggs reserved for older people were made using darker colors.

FORTY TRIANGLES

The forty triangles on this egg represent the many facets of life; for example, family matters such as the birth of children, weddings, and travel, farming, animal husbandry and strength. The magic number three enclosed the wish or prayer for each special area of life. In Christian times, forty triangles represented the forty days of Lent, the forty days of Christ's fasting and the forty martyrs.

CIRCLES

According to Ukrainian tradition, the simple form of a circle is the most significant and powerful symbol for protection known to exist. The miracle of the circle is in its shape. Evil cannot penetrate that which has no beginning and no end. Circles and belts were also tied in with spring dances and games, peace, love and goodness. Eggs decorated with many belts were used as protection from family betrayal. Old women cast benevolent spells using belted eggs to help unloved people become loved.

SKY, SUN, MOON, STARS

In this *pysanka*, the sun sends out rays from the top of the egg to the moon which is represented in the bottom. Between the rays are the limitless stars. This old design symbolizes begging the sun to give its healing warmth to the earth and entreats it not to burn the crops. The moon is begged to shed its light at night to help the traveler and to chase away evil powers from the household.

TREE

In pysanky designs, leaves and branches can represent whole trees and even forests. The rich folklore of old Ukraine often represents trees as people. Men are oaks, maples or beech trees. Women are represented by birch, poplar and bass wood trees. The trees have adventures and lessons from which everyone can learn. For folk medicine, bass wood flowers are gathered, dried and made into a tea to promote good health. Bark and acorns were gathered from the oak, cooked in water and cooled, and then used to bathe a sick child to make him as strong as an oak. Trees have a universal meaning for long life, good health, strength and youthfulness.

VINOK (GARLAND)

A *vinok* is the beautiful garland of flowers which is most often worn by girls and maidens around their heads during holidays and celebrations.

Vinky originated in pre-Christian times and in poetry it symbolized the girl's desire for freedom. As a national ornament, the *vinok* is in first place as a beloved symbol. On *pysanky*, *vinky* are drawn in three circles around the egg. One on the pointed end, one in the middle and one around the wide end of the egg. Each *vinok* represents a wish for the three parts of human existence: birth, marriage, and life. These *pysanky* are so popular, they have a special name, "Vinochok"

Gate eggs are given primarily to older people for they represent the gates of heaven. Lines are drawn from the top to the bottom of the egg with branches going in alternate directions.

HEAVENLY GATE EGGS

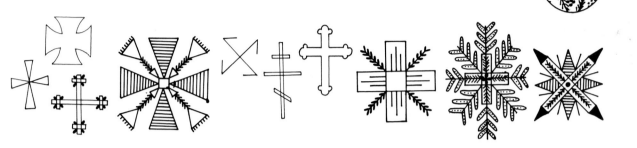

The ancient sandscrit symbol for good luck, was the four spoked solar wheel, or a swastica. Endless variations of crosses were drawn on *pysanky* in pagan times to symbolize the four corners of the earth. With newer Christian beliefs, the meanings gradually represented Christ's great gift to man kind, His crucifixtion and resurrection.

CROSSES

In pagan times, grapes were once the sign of a good harvest. As Christianity spread across Ukraine, the old meanings changed and grapes came to stand for the growing church.

GRAPES

A symbol of hard work and pleasantness, bees represent all good insects which should not be killed. In Ukrainian folklore and life, a bee is treated with honor and respect. For example, if one sees a bee floundering in water, he should rescue the bee and allow it to dry in the warm sun. Bees are held in such esteem that Ukrainians have a special verb to describe the death of a bee (*zahynula*). Bees provide ample wax and honey for the people and pollenate crops.

BEES

39

SNAKE

A snake *had* is a creature with mystical powers which should not be confused with a snake that bites us. In folklore, a *had* is a small harmless grey snake which is commonly found by every village house. (Bad people did not have a *had*) The presence of the snake protects all the people living in the house. This symbol on *pysanky* brought protection from catastrophy.

FISH

Before Christianity, the fish represented a mystical creature of action. In fairy tales, fish helped the hero to win his fight with evil. And in songs, fish helped people to find their way out of confusion. With the introduction of Christianity, the fish symbolized Christ. The Greek alphabet spells the word "Fish" from "Jesus Christ Son of God Savior" (Ichthys). It was the sign of recognition among early Christians.

WATER

Water is represented with two or three waves in symmetrical order. The design has traditionally meant providing wealth since there can be no harvest without rain.

In this century, the meaning of the water symbol has changed to represent separation for many Ukrainian young people who immigrated to the United States and Canada. As a parting gift, mothers gave a *pysanka* with the water symbol to their children. The waving lines now began to represent the great waters of the Atlantic Ocean. The interpretation of the symbol exists in the mind of the artist, and as times change, the meanings also change.

A whole series of eggs were designed to "call spring". Patterns using water and flowers, growing plants and little wings were drawn on *pysanky* to summon nature to be reborn.

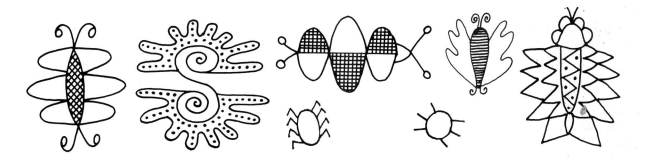

Circles with short lines extending from them represented the sun and/or insects and even sometimes the branches of trees. They are used to signify the sound of spring, to "call spring", and to praise it. The designs represent birds singing, crickets and the chirping noise of the forest itself. These are called "noise insect eggs" in Ukranian.

SPRING SOUND EGGS

A meander line meanders or moves around the egg in a predictable pattern. It has no beginning and no ending, and like the circle, it represents eternity and everlasting life.

All of nature follows predictable cycles: celestial movements, changing tides, day and night, seasons and the cycles of life. Nature has its own meander patterns which the artist symbolizes with rythmic lines.

MEANDER LINES

Here is a collection of border designs. Feast your eyes on the colorful symmetry.

NETS During pagan times the net represented knowledge and mother-hood. After Christianity was accepted in Ukraine, the crisscross design symbolized Christ's reference to his followers to become "fishers of men".

3 BANDED EGGS Three belts were drawn on the egg first. Three pronged figures with spiraled ends were drawn between them and the design used three colors, red for the sun, yellow for happiness of life and green for the rebirth of nature in the never ending world. These *pysanky* were used for many spring games as well as representing peace, love and goodness.

Summary: Symbols and Traditions

In Pre-Christian times, *pysanky* were closely tied with the customs and viewpoints of the Ukrainian people. *Pysanky* were used for fortune telling, healing, witchcraft and other mystical rites. The unique history of the *pysanky* is an echo of a distant people who respected nature and who worked hard to survive. The designs were intimately related to the greeting of spring, a holiday where life won out over death.

Since *pysanky* were not expensive to make, even the poorest home had eggs for the coming Easter holiday. They were an art form available to all and indeed, often the poorer family could produce a stunning collection if the egg makers had special talents.

Uses of *pysanky* reflect the philosophy of protection. For example, when constructing a new home, the four corners were marked with decorated eggs which were buried in the ground; then the house was built. The house was believed to be protected from evil spirits. When a young woman got married, she took a *pysanky* to the ceremony and carried it in her skirt. Afterwards, when she arrived home, she let the egg drop from her skirt while saying quietly, "Let me bear the child as easily as the egg falls."

When a baby was born, the neighbors included *pysanka* with their gifts of honey and milk, for they wished the child to be as round and as smooth as an egg.

References to *pysanky* are found interwoven throughout national creativity: songs, customs, sayings and folk tales. The symbols used in the designs have very deep meanings and have gradually developed over the centuries since it is an art form which is fluid and ever-changing. The slow evolution of symbols has been assisted by the many thousands of artisans, past and present.

Ten Ways to Divide an Egg

For variety in design,
10 basic divisions
for beginning a pattern
are suggested.

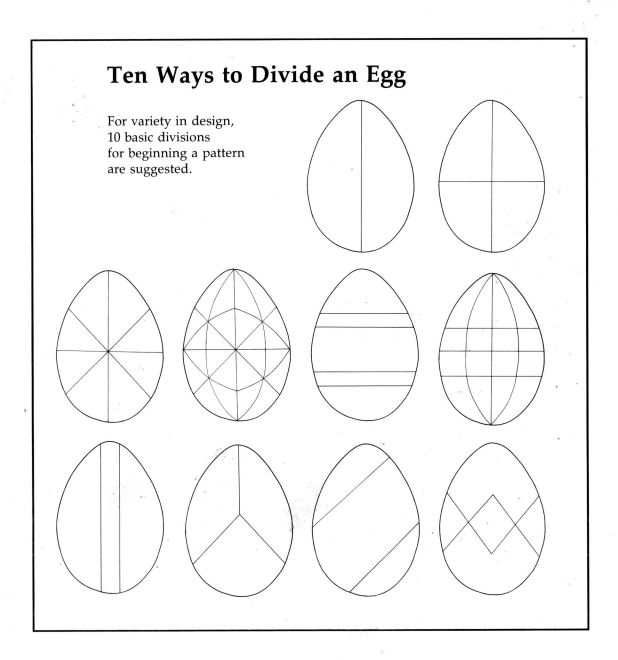

Even though Ukrainian tradition
dictates a geometric balance
in designing the tips on *pysanky,*
the possibilities of variations
in the designs are limitless.

CHAPTER 3

How to Make a Pysanka

M aterials needed: Eggs, kistka, bees wax, dyes, candle, spoons, soft cloth, tissues, paper towel, pencil, paintbrush, or cotton swabs, varnish, and hand soap, cleaning fluid, melting rack, working area. Optional materials: egg lathe, rubber band, black felt tipped pen (permanant ink).

EGGS Choose smooth, fresh eggs for making *pysanky*. If the eggs need to be washed, they should be rinsed in a solution of one quart of tepid water mixed with ¼ cup of white vinegar. Gently blot them dry with a clean cloth or tissue. The vinegar-water solution is used because a detergent or soap tends to leave a residue on the shell.

Allow the eggs to come to room temperature before they are decorated. Cold eggs from the refrigerator will "sweat", causing problems with the wax application.

Look for hair-line cracks and weak spots in the shell by holding the egg up to a light. Eggs with a noticeable flaw should not be used. Only firm-shelled, symmetrical eggs should be used for *pysanky*.

Not only chicken eggs, but goose, rhea, and even ostrich eggs can be decorated in the Ukrainian batik fashion. The latter three are usually blown before they are purchased. The ends of blown eggs can be sealed with candle wax and decorated in the same way as fresh eggs, except they must be held down in the dye when they are dipped.

**KISTKY
(WRITING TOOL)** The kistka, or writing tool, comes in a variety of styles and sizes. Some are hand made and some are made by machine. Basically, a kistka is a funnel attached to a stick. Wax is scooped into the funnel,

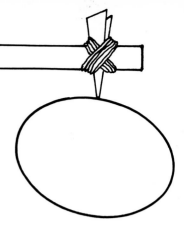

heated, and then the tool is drawn across the egg for a smooth wax line. Kistky may be purchased in sizes ranging from very fine to heavy, depending on the needs of the artist. It is usually a good idea to purchase at least two or three kistky for variety in the wax designs,

Electric kistky are available throughout the United States and Canada. They can be classified into two main types: The stationary tip and the interchangable tip.

The stationary tip electric kistka may be purchased at a reasonable price and comes in several sizes. Each kistka writes with one width of wax line, so if the artist wishes to have another size line, he must purchase other kistky or varying sizes. Two or three kistky work quite well. These kistky rarely drip and are comfortable to use for long periods of time.

The interchangable electric kistka works well and has the added advantage of allowing the artist to change the tips when a different width of line is needed. These kistky are somewhat more expensive.

Both types offer faster, smoother writing than the traditional kistka and are extremely popular.

ELECTRIC KISTKY

A candle on a secure holder is needed to heat the traditional kistka. The candle should not be too tall or the decorator must keep reaching up. If the decorator is right handed, the candle should be placed on

CANDLE

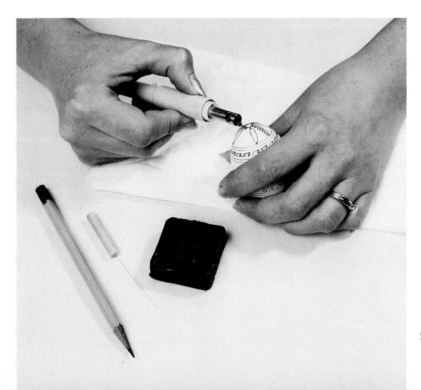

When working with the electric kistka, some people find it convenient to keep the wax fluid. This electric wax warmer is kept hot with two small light bulbs.

Stationery tip electric kistka

the right side and visa versa to simplify the egg decorating process. Some artists also use a candle to melt the wax from the egg at the end of the process.

BEESWAX

Beeswax has a high melting point which allows it to flow without smearing or smudging. Candle wax or paraffin will not give the same clear effect, so they are not used. Regular pure beeswax is needed for the non-electric kistka. This wax gradually becomes black because of the carbon in the flame. Two ounce cakes last for many eggs since only a small amount is needed to decorate each one. Place the wax between yourself and the candle for convenience as you work.

Darkened beeswax must be used with the electric kistka because of the absence of carbon. Otherwise, it is difficult to see the lines you are drawing. If there is none available, we suggest two possible solutions:

First, melt two ounces of beeswax in a tin can which is placed in a pan of hot water (not boiling). As the wax melts, add either a half piece of black crayon or a half teaspoon of black shoe polish to turn the beeswax black. Because beeswax is flamable, it should be heated slowly.

The second method requires cooking the beeswax for several hours until it turns black by itself. An old electric cooker works well for this method.

After the beeswax has been colored black by either method, carefully pour it into small paper cups to cool. Later, peel off the paper and use the cakes of dark wax for the electric kistka.

DYES

Analine dyes are strong, modern colors, ideal for making Ukrainian *pysanky*. However, they should not be used to color eggs that are to be eaten beacuse they are a chemical rather than vegetable dye. The colors available are yellow, orange, red, blue, green, black, brown, purple, pink, dark red, turquoise, wine, royal blue, brick brown and dark green. For the beginner, we suggest six basic colors: yellow, orange, red, green, blue and black. Other colors may be used according to personal preference.

Mix the dyes with boiling water according to the directions on the package and allow to cool. If vinegar is to be added, use only white vinegar, but be sure to read the directions carefully since some colors do not require it. Mix the dyes in clean, wide mouth jars (salad dressing and peanut butter jars are good). Dyes will be at their best if

they are fresh for each season. Vinegar may be added occasionally to dyes which require it. The vinegar strengthens the dye for several days.

A suggested set up for the working area with all the materials close at hand.

One spoon is needed for each color dye. Choose a tablespoon because it is large enough to hold the egg securely when dipping. Plastic spoons are not strong enough for this purpose.

SPOONS

A simple rack made from nails and a piece of wood is used both to melt the wax and to varnish the egg. Nails are pounded into a board in the form of triangles to hold each egg. Heavy cardboard may be used instead of wood.

EGG RACK

Cover a table with a few layers of newspaper. The egg is placed on tissue so it will not become smudged from the newsprint. Set up a

WORKING AREA

53

desk lamp so the light is comfortable for your eyes and also so there is no shadow which obstructs the view of the egg. Have paper towels handy for each color dye, so that they can be reused. It saves money and clutter to let the towels dry, and use them again.

Sit up straight with both feet on the floor. It is much more comfortable and easier on you.

SOFT CLOTH OR TISSUE Cloths are used to wipe the wax from the egg in the final step. The tissue or paper towels are placed beneath the egg while working and for blotting the dye from the egg.

VARNISH & HAND SOAP At the hardware store, purchase a small can of clear liquid varnish for finishing the eggs; and a can of commericial hand soap to clean your hands afterwards.

CLEANING FLUID We recommend using cleaning fluid to remove an unwanted drop of wax or a mistake. First scrape the wax off with your fingernail. Slightly dampen a cotton swab with cleaning fluid. and carefully clean the area, making sure all wax is removed. Then continue applying wax to your design.

PENCIL When dividing the egg in white, a pencil is used to draw the lines *lightly*. The pencil lines do not show later, and they help to insure a more balanced design. The most experienced egg makers use pencil lines for their divisions. Never erase pencil lines or the dye will not take to the shell.

PAINT BRUSH OR COTTON SWAB To add touches of color with blue or green, a paint brush or cotton swab is included in the list of materials used.

RUBBER BAND A wide rubber band may be used to help draw straight lines around the egg.

EGG LATHE Egg lathes have been used to take the guess work out of measuring and making horizontal lines around the egg.

BLACK FELT TIPPED PEN If you think you may have some unwanted spots on the *pysanka*, dip the egg into the black dye for the last color. Melt the wax and then repair the spots with the black felt tip pen (permanent ink). This little hint works very well.

Application of Basic Lines

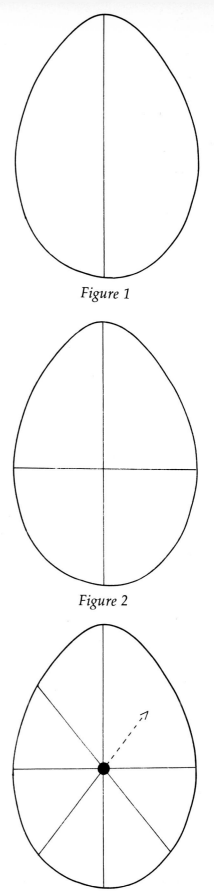

Figure 1

Place your arms on the table holding the egg on a paper towel. Starting at the top of the egg, hold the lead pencil steady in one hand and rotate the egg in the other making a light line lengthwise.

Again at the top, draw another light line across the first line at right angles. The egg will now be divided into quarters as shown in figure 1.

Now draw a horizontal line around the middle of the egg dividing the egg into eight equal parts, as shown in figure 2. Remember *never* erase pencil marks on the shell because erasers will cause smudging.

The next step is to draw diagonal lines beginning at the center; with a long stroke, divide each section again forming a basic pattern with eight divisions on each side of the egg as seen in figure 3.

These lines are drawn to give you a framework from which to form your full design. You are now ready to apply the wax to the design. With the heated kistka, cover the pencil lines with long strokes. Try to relax your hand and not press the tool into the shell.

Figure 2

Figure 3

Next, draw a small circle in the center and fill it in with wax. For a more balanced design, if you wish, using a light pencil line, divide each section one more time as seen in figure 4.

Using the pencil line as a guide, center the pedal in each section as seen in figure 5.

Place the egg on a spoon and ease it into the yellow dye. In approximately five to ten minutes (or until desired shade) the egg may be removed from the dye and patted dry with a clean tissue. Do not rub.

On the yellow egg, apply wax lines at the end of the pedal as seen in figure 6.

To apply green, use a small brush or cotton swab. Dip the swab into the green or blue dye and make a dot at the end of the branch. Blot dry with a clean tissue. See figure 7. Then apply wax over the green dot. The orange dye will rinse away any green color not covered with wax.

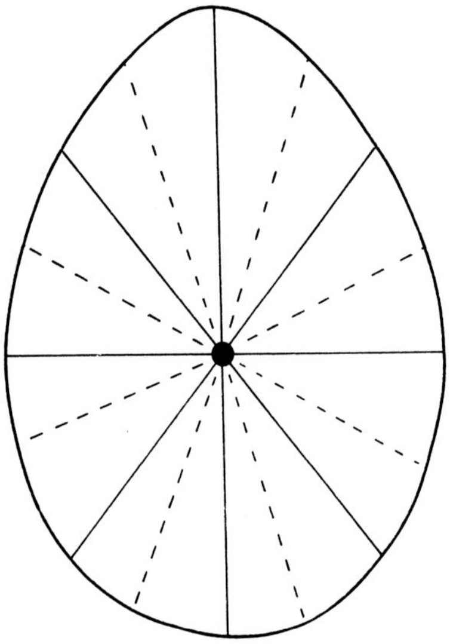

Figure 4

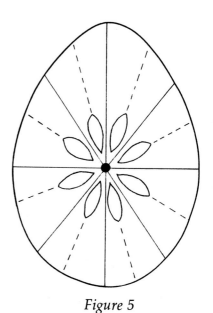

Figure 5

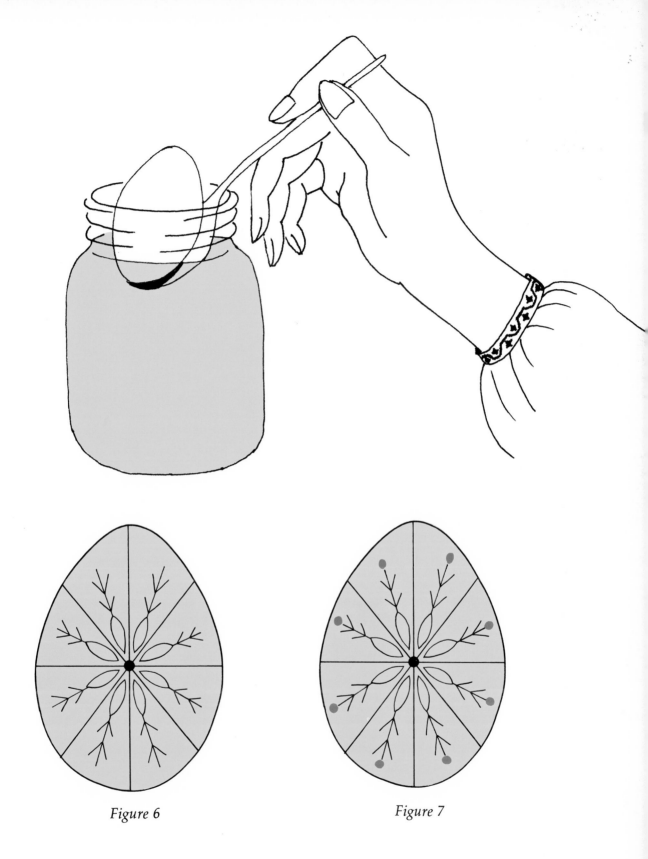

Figure 6

Figure 7

Figure 8

Figure 9

Now dip the egg into the orange dye. When the desired color is reached, pat dry with a clean tissue. With a kistka, apply wax dots to the ends of the branches and short lines in each pedal as seen in figure 8.

Then dip the egg into the red dye. Pat dry. Using the heavier kistka, fill in the pedals solidly with wax making sure there are no spaces left uncovered. Now draw a dot on each branch as seen in figure 9.

Next dip the egg into the black dye leaving it until a rich solid black has been absorbed on the shell. This may take from ten to thirty minutes. Remove and blot dry. You are through applying the design to the egg. Allow the egg to dry thoroughly (15 minutes) before removing the wax.

Removing wax can be done in several ways. We often melt the wax using the flame of the candle. This is done by slowly moving the egg back and forth in the side of the flame until the section looks wet (2 to 5 seconds) as seen in figure 10. Then, with a clean soft cloth, wipe off the wax as shown in figure 11. This is where you will begin to see all the work you have done. Be careful not to hold the egg *over* the flame because carbon will collect on the shell and darken the design. Do not attempt to heat too large a portion of the egg at one time. After you have finished melting all the wax, blow out the candle,

Figure 10

and gently wipe the egg with a tissue dipped in a small amount of cleaning fluid to remove any carbon or wax that may still be on the shell. It is important to have a clean shell before varnishing!

Figure 11

When melting a larger number of eggs, use the oven method. The egg rack is placed into a preheated oven set at 180° farenheit. Heat the eggs gently for fifteen to twenty minutes, keeping the oven door open. Check from time to time so that the eggs do not become too hot. When they are warm and look glossy, take them out, one at a time, and wipe off the melted wax with a clean, soft cloth. Place the eggs in a bowl or a carton and allow them to cool.

Varnishing the eggs may be done in the following manner. Have ready: newspaper, varnish, hand soap and paper towels. Spread the newspapers and open a small can of clear gloss varnish. With your fingers, gently apply varnish to each egg. Be sure you have covered the entire shell with a thin coat and then place it on the rack to dry. It will take several hours.

To clean the varnish from your hands, first wipe the excess varnish from your hands on to a paper towel. Then clean hands with the paint soap which is not harsh to the skin.

The decorated egg, though fragile, will keep for many years, long after its contents have dried out. Turn the eggs over every few months, for this will allow the egg to dry out evenly.

CHAPTER 4

Suggested Designs

We have collected nine easy, nine intermediate and nine more difficult eggs (pages 62, 63 and 64). Step by step diagrams for each egg offers a good variety of designs for the serious beginner. Some eggs are only dipped twice while others may be dipped up to five times.

The finished eggs will be ready to be melted and varnished. Each individual egg has a suggested final color. However, you may choose any background you prefer.

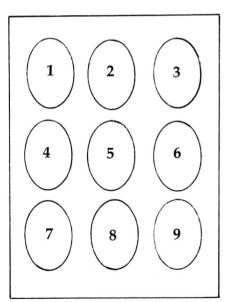

Page 62

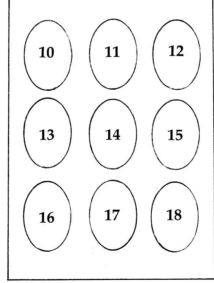

Page 63

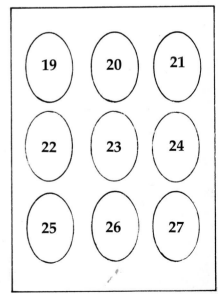

Page 64

White

The first drawing shows the design that should be applied to the white egg.

Yellow

This drawing shows the lines that should be added to the design after the egg has been dipped into the yellow dye.

Pink, Purple Background

The added lines here should be applied over the third color, pink.

Purple is suggested for the final background color.

66

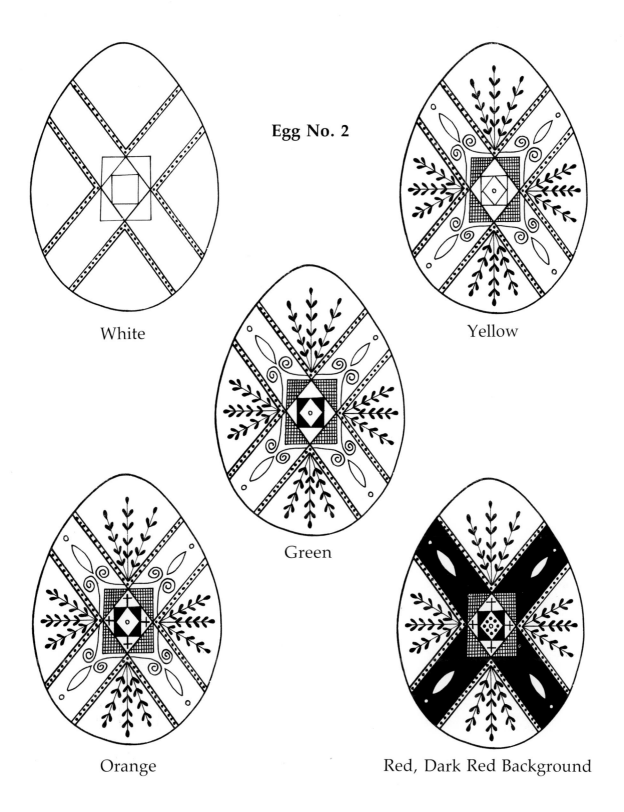

Egg No. 2

White

Yellow

Green

Orange

Red, Dark Red Background

Egg No. 3

White   Red, Black Background

Egg No. 4

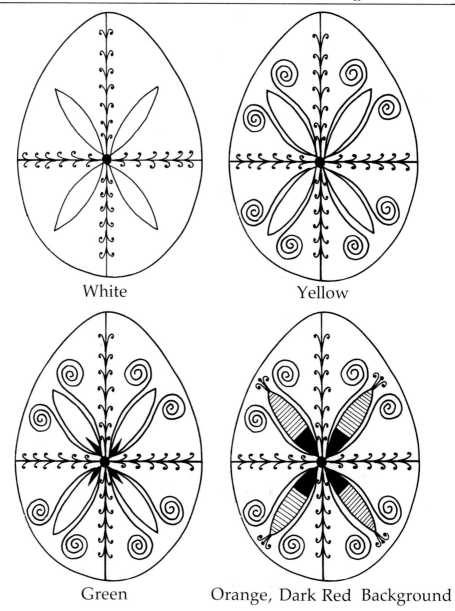

White   Yellow

Green   Orange, Dark Red Background

68

Egg No. 5

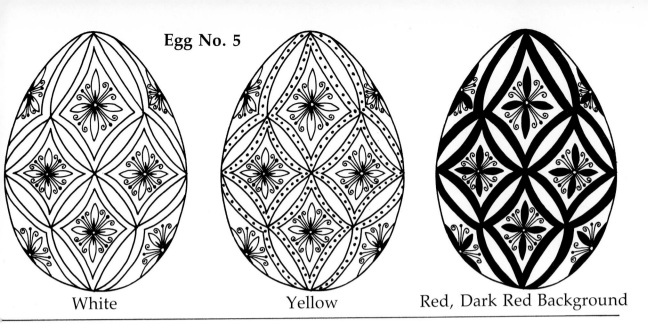

White   Yellow   Red, Dark Red Background

Egg No. 6

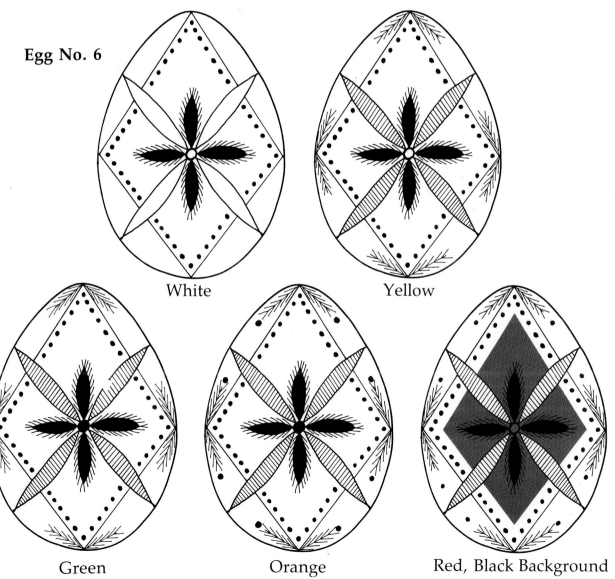

White   Yellow

Green   Orange   Red, Black Background

Egg No. 7

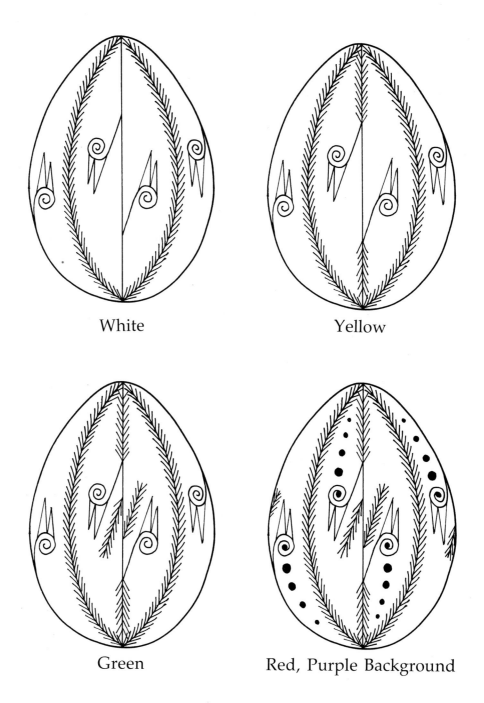

White

Yellow

Green

Red, Purple Background

Egg No. 8

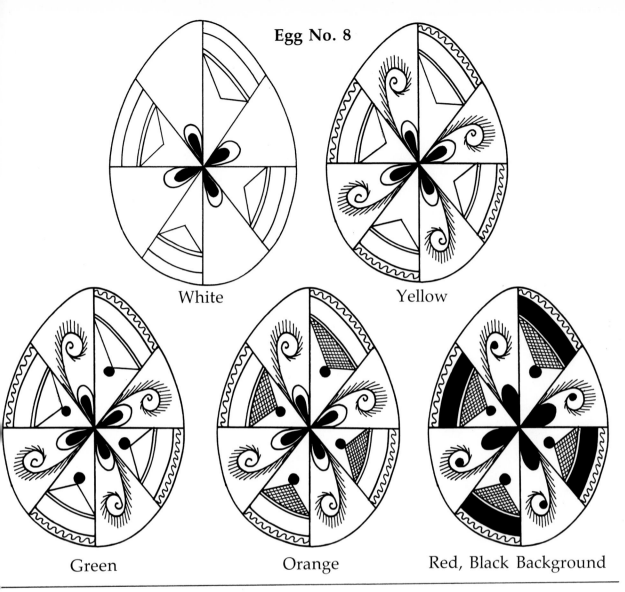

White

Yellow

Green

Orange

Red, Black Background

Egg No. 9

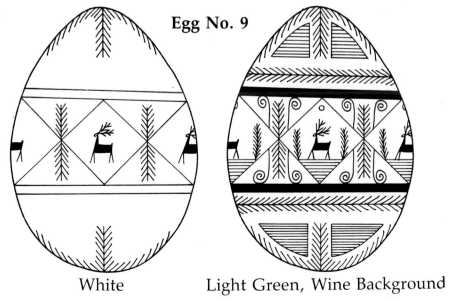

White

Light Green, Wine Background

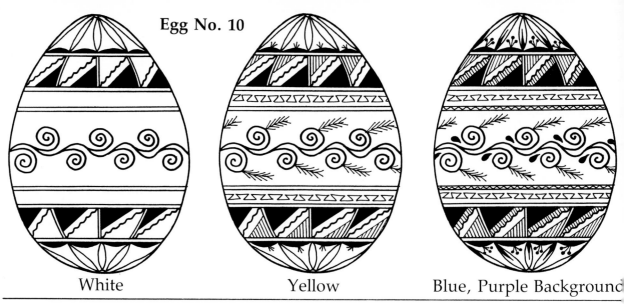

Egg No. 10

White   Yellow   Blue, Purple Background

Egg No. 11

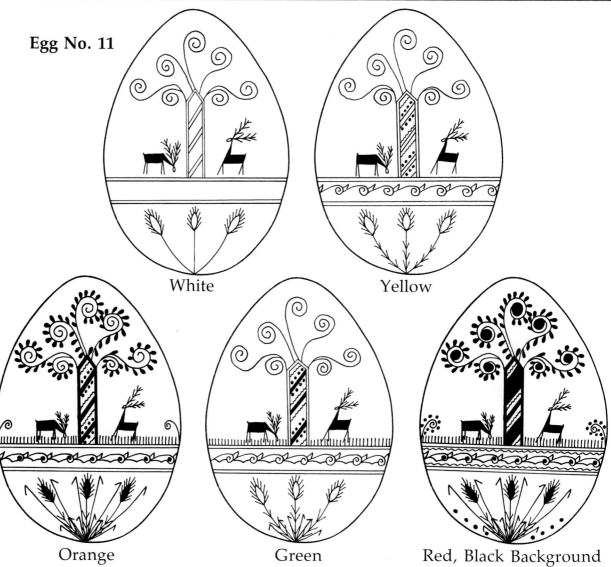

White   Yellow

Orange   Green   Red, Black Background

72

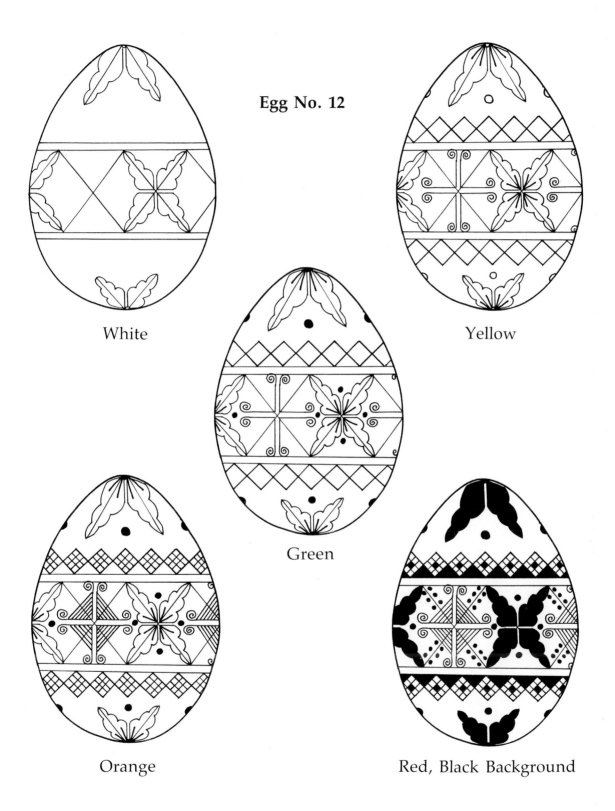

Egg No. 12

White

Yellow

Green

Orange

Red, Black Background

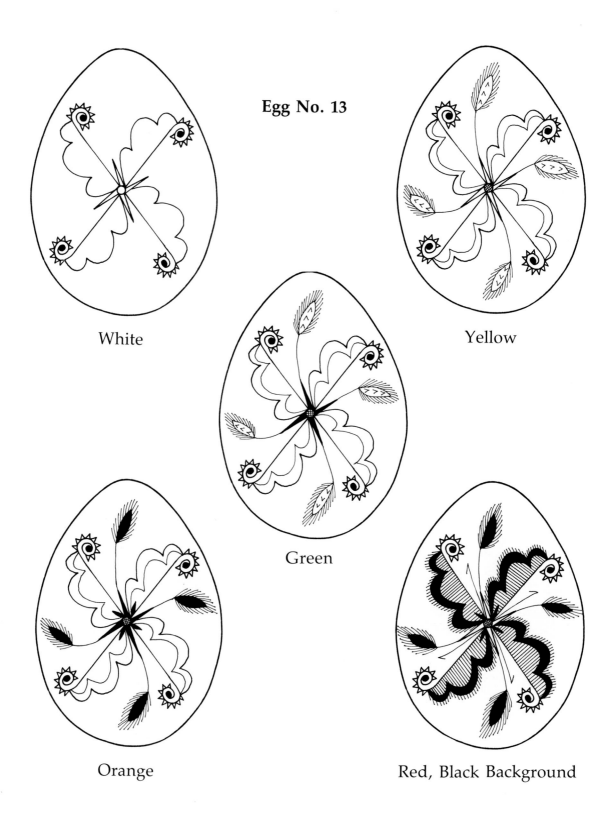

Egg No. 13

White

Yellow

Green

Orange

Red, Black Background

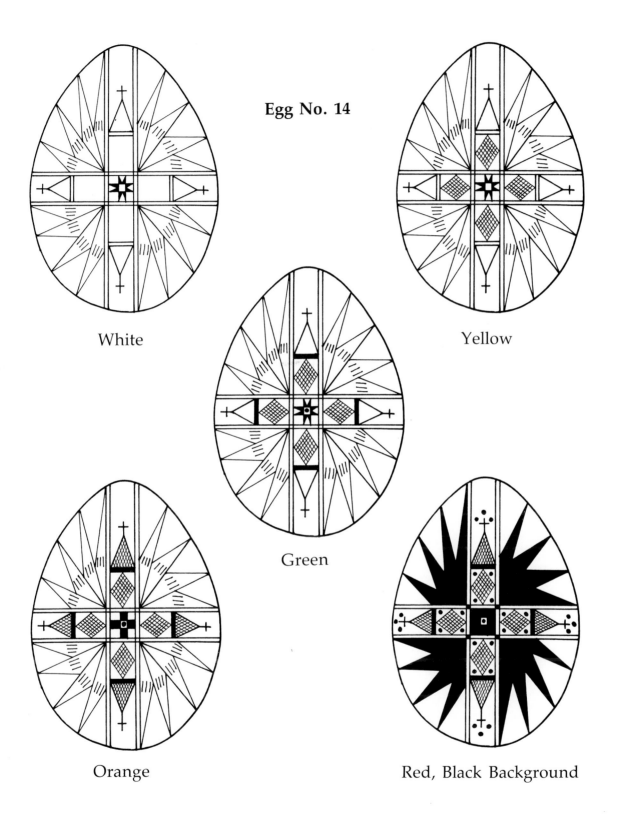

Egg No. 14

White

Yellow

Green

Orange

Red, Black Background

Egg No. 15

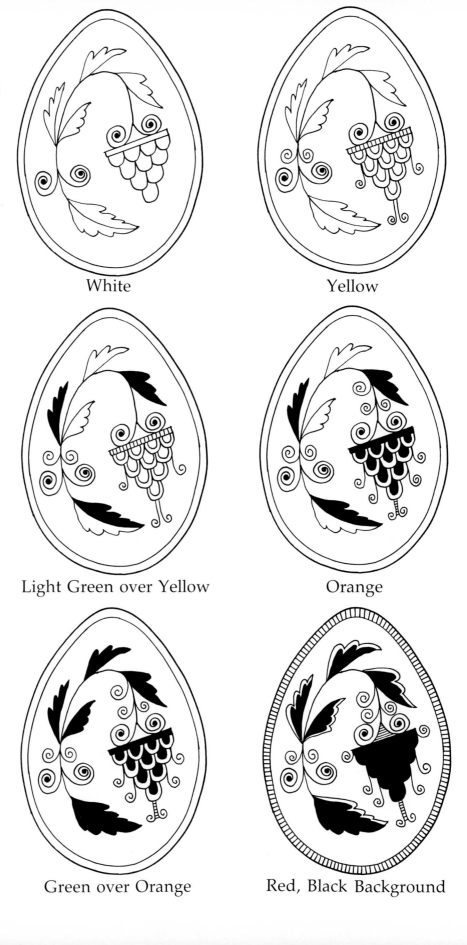

White

Yellow

Light Green over Yellow

Orange

Green over Orange

Red, Black Background

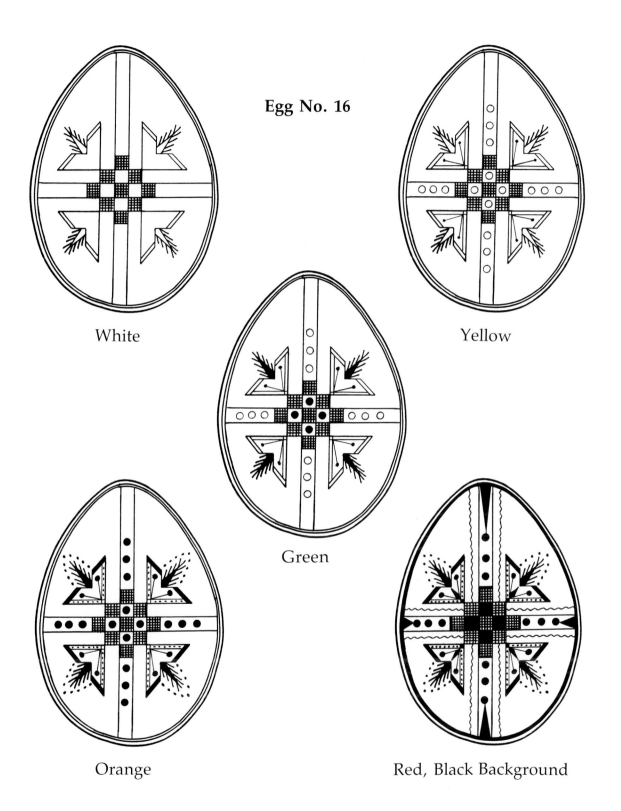

Egg No. 16

White

Yellow

Green

Orange

Red, Black Background

77

Egg No. 17

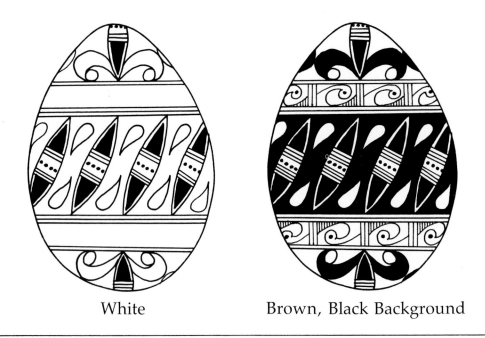

White   Brown, Black Background

Egg No. 18

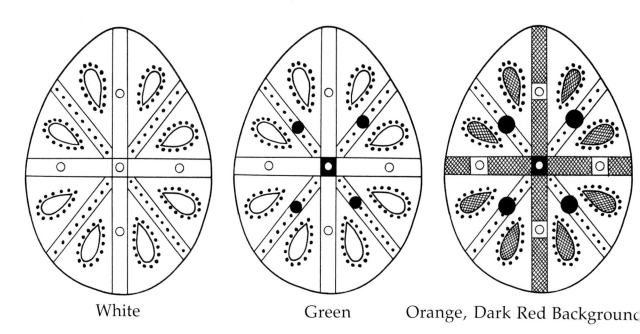

White   Green   Orange, Dark Red Background

Egg No. 19

White

Yellow

Green

Orange

Red, Dark Red Background

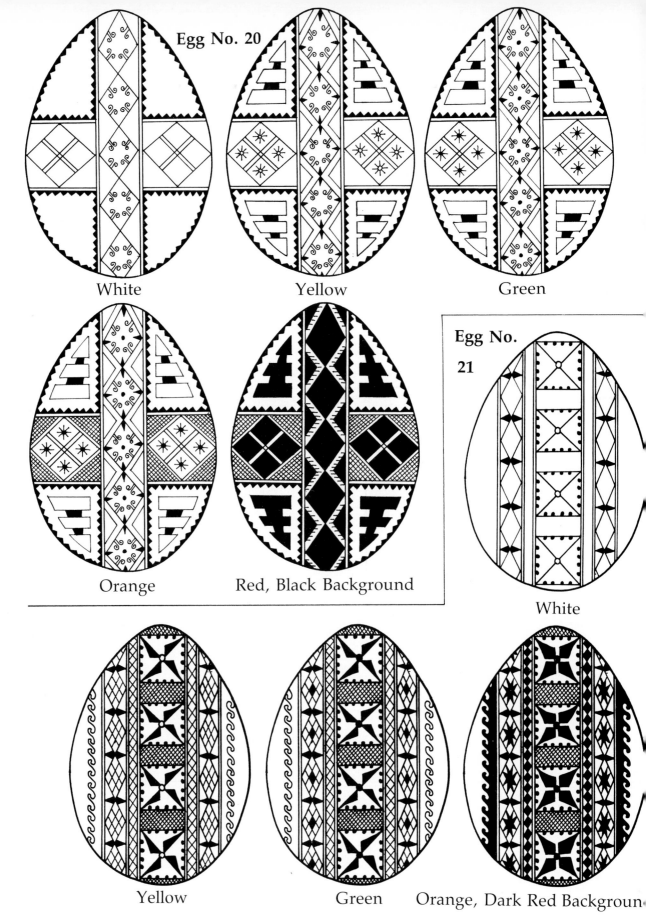

Egg No. 20

White

Yellow

Green

Orange

Red, Black Background

Egg No. 21

White

Yellow

Green

Orange, Dark Red Background

80

Egg No. 22

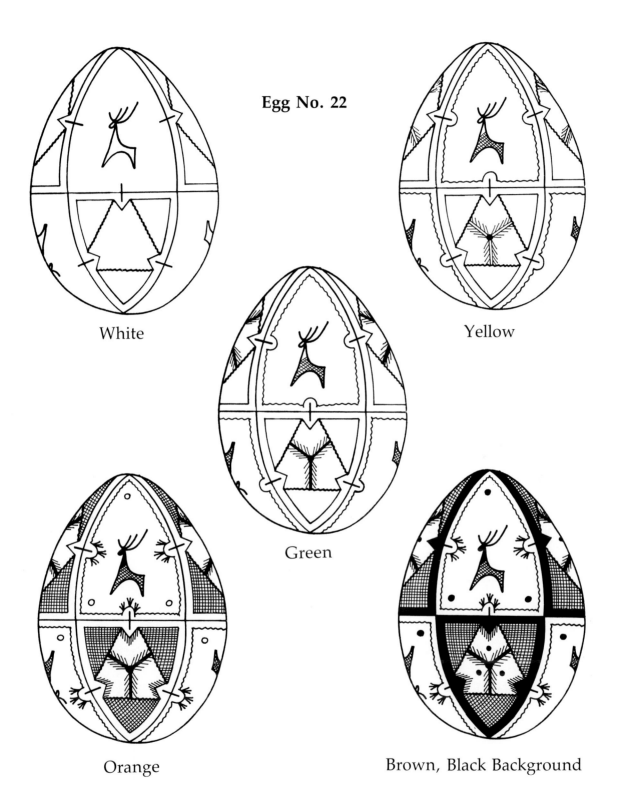

White

Yellow

Green

Orange

Brown, Black Background

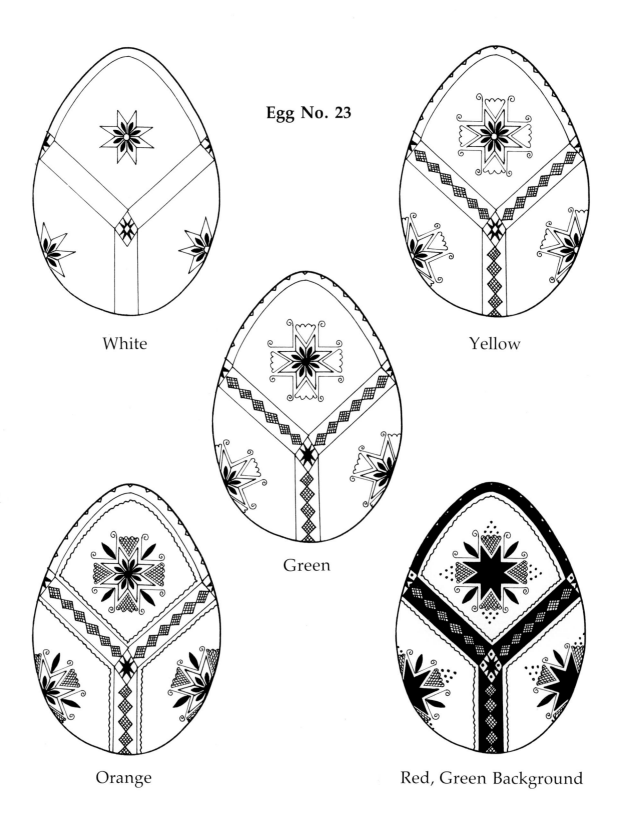

Egg No. 23

White

Yellow

Green

Orange

Red, Green Background

82

Egg No. 24

White

Yellow

Green

Orange

Red, Black Background

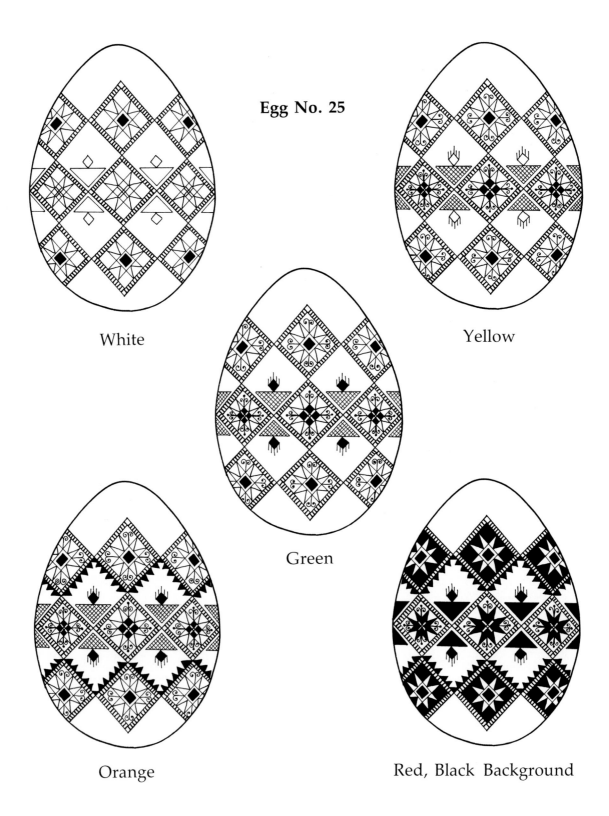

Egg No. 25

White

Yellow

Green

Orange

Red, Black Background

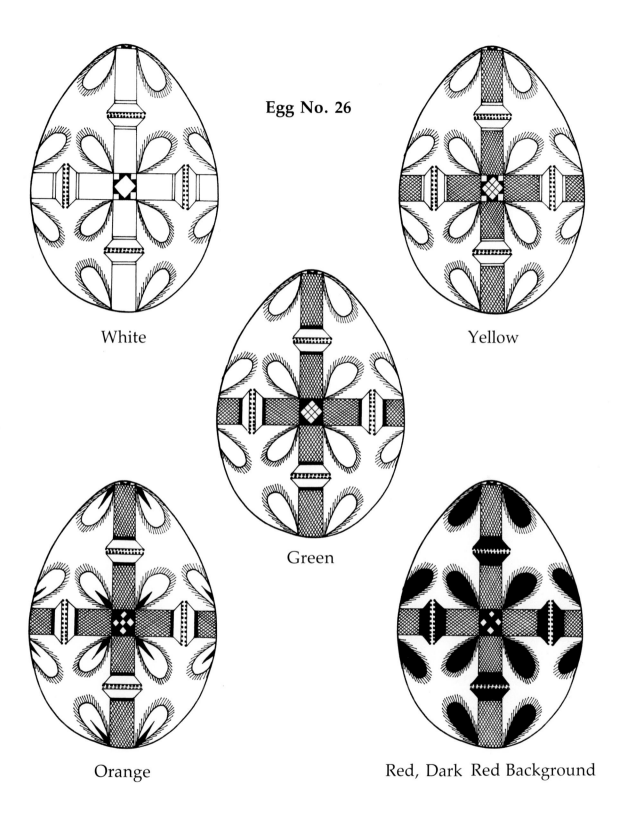

Egg No. 26

White

Yellow

Green

Orange

Red, Dark Red Background

Egg No. 27

White

Yellow

Green

Orange

Red, Black Background

CHAPTER 5

Color Combinations and Techniques

T he customary sequences of colors (from lighter to darker) in decorating Ukrainian *pysanky* can be varied to produce eggs with unusual beauty and color. After many years of personal successes and failures at color combinations, we offer this information to the readers who would like to try unusual effects.

ORANGE DYE

Have an extra orange dye on hand and use it only to rinse out darker colors. Orange dye can rinse out greens, blues, reds and browns. After using the orange rinse, you can go into a completely different color scheme.

WATER RINSE

A small jar of water (room temperature) can be kept on hand. If you have a dark blue egg, you may soak the egg in water until it has lightened to a lighter blue. Dry the egg with a tissue and add wax to the lighter blue before dipping the egg into another color for two blues. When using the rinse, check the egg from time to time to be sure you get the desired color. You may want to leave light blue for the last color or continue dipping the egg into purple or red dyes for interesting effects.

BLEACHING

If a white background is desired, a different sequence of color is used on the egg. For example, the egg is FIRST dipped into a dye (yellow, orange or red) and then the basic design is drawn in that color. Afterwards, the egg goes into lighter or darker colors, depending on the desired effect.

To create the final white background, stop before melting the wax. Gently wash the egg in a solution of two tablespoons bleach in one cup of cool water. After the naked shell has become completely white, rinse the bleached egg under cool running water. When the egg no longer feels slippery, wipe with a tissue. Important: allow the egg to dry at least ½ hour before melting the wax from the shell.

You may try these possible sequences:
1. yellow, red, blue and bleach
2. orange, blue and bleach
3. pink, blue, bleach
4. red, orange, yellow, bleach

BROWN EGGS

Unusual *pysanky*, also come from using the many delicate shades of brown eggs for the first color, rather than only choosing white eggs. Designs of subdued and earthy colors are the result of this method and it is worth your time to work with brown eggs for special "old fashioned" effects. We find brown eggs made with browns, orange and black dyes are extremely dramatic.

The Simple Drop-Pull Method of Batik

MATERIALS NEEDED

1. smooth, fresh eggs at room temperature
2. writing tools, straight common pins with heads of various sizes, firmly stuck into wooden dowels or in the eraser of a pencil.
3. wax mixture — ½ beeswax and ½ parafin wax
4. wax warmer — either an electric one or a candle heated device to keep the wax hot and flowing
5. dyes — several bright water soluble colors
6. paper tissues to wipe the eggs dry
7. newspaper — to cover the table

DIRECTIONS

Divide the white egg in half, fourths and eights with light pencil lines as shown on page 55. Be sure the wax mixtures is hot. (Please be careful with the hot wax because it is flammable) Place the wax as close to your working area as possible so you will not lose too much heat as you apply wax to the egg. If desired, you may practice on paper before beginning to work on the egg.

The drop-pull method requires quick work. To make a dot, dip the pin head of the tool into the hot wax and touch the egg quickly. To make the tear drop shape, draw the pin along the surface of the egg. You must dip the pin head into the hot beeswax for each dot or drop shape.

After the white design has been completed with the wax, dip the egg into the first dye, usually a light color such as yellow or orange. When the desired color has been obtained, remove the egg from the dye (10-30 minutes). Blot dry and add more tear drops or dots to the design with melted wax.

These eggs may be varnished and kept raw or may be varnished and blown upon completion.

It is possible to blow eggs before decorating them. The liquid egg may be used for cooking and the empty shell is then rinsed and sealed with a small amount of wax at the opening. The blown eggs must be held under the dye with a heavier object, but otherwise, the procedure is the same as with whole eggs.

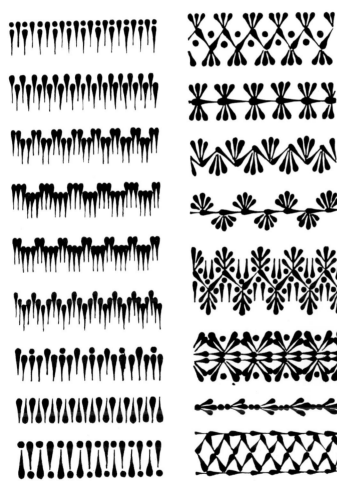

Suggested drop-pull designs

Simple dots and tear drop shapes are combined to make designs of primitive beauty.

Usually only two or three colors are used for this batik style of decoration. Progress from the lighter to the darker colors. For example, go from white to yellow, orange and then have red for the final color. Another popular sequence of color would be white, blue and purple.

To Make the "Stained Glass" Type of Design

MATERIALS NEEDED

several white eggs, blown
black beeswax
regular or electric kistka
very fine paint brush
ordinary Easter egg dyes or India ink
in several colors

The complete design is drawn on the white egg with the dark wax. With the brush, fill in small areas of the design with one color on one side of the egg. Allow to dry thoroughly. You will find that you must wait until the dye dries before continuing to apply more colors. The wax will not be removed from the egg.

When all the colors have been applied to the egg, paint clear nail polish on one half of the egg and allow to dry for at least ½ hour. Then paint the other side with polish. (Varnish is not recommended for this type of egg.)

The wax resist method can be used on pullet, chicken, goose, rhea and ostrich eggs.

How to Blow Out Eggs:

After varnishing the finished *pysanky*, eggs may also be blown. However, the insides of these eggs cannot be used for cooking. If you plan to blow your eggs, do not remove the wax with the oven method because the eggs may partially cook while warming and it would not be possible to thoroughly remove the insides. We recommend removing the wax with the candle and/or cleaning fluid. The newly made *pysanka* is still a fresh egg and it is best to blow the egg at that time.

Three different methods for blowing eggs are popular. First, use either a fine drill or a long pin and make a neat hole at each end of the egg: a smaller hole at the top and a hole about ⅛ inch wide at the bottom. With a long pin, pierce and break the yolk inside. Shake the egg vigorously to mix up the inner contents. Hold the egg over a bowl. Blow through the smaller top hole to force the contents out of the large hole. It is somewhat difficult but practice helps and you will find yourself a professional after several eggs! Immediately after emptying, rinse the shell out with water and prop it on paper towels or an egg carton to dry.

The second method we have used to blow eggs requires purchasing a special syringe tool from a craft shop especially designed for this purpose. It is easier to blow the eggs with the inexpensive tool and only one hole needs to be made in the shell.

The third method requires practice on eating eggs first! A hypodermic needle can be used to extract the contents of the egg. One hole is made at the bottom of the shell and it works reasonably well to gradually withdraw the contents this way.

Hanging Eggs

If you wish to suspend a *pysanka*, as the Ukrainian peasants did in their homes and barns, the following method is suggested.

Tie a long length of narrow ribbon, cord or thread to the middle of a wooden

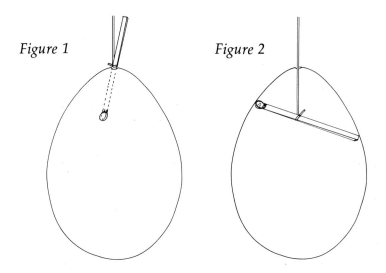

Figure 1   *Figure 2*

matchstick. A small amount of glue may be smeared on the stick where the thread is tied to keep it from slipping. Carefully, insert the matchstick straight down into the largest hole (figure 1). The stick will become wedged crosswise inside the shell and will not pull out (figure 2).

Information on Purchasing Materials

Contact your local Ukrainian store for supplies, or write to:

> The Ukrainian Gift Shop
> 2242 Central Avenue, N.E.
> Minneapolis, MN 55418

Added Tips for Egg Decorators

First, we cannot remind you too much, you will have the best results with your *pysanky* if you:

1. Use only fresh eggs with good firm shells
2. Keep the finished *pysanka* out of the sun
3. Do not store *pysanky* in a tight place
   (A plastic carton or a china cabinet which has tightly closed doors inhibits normal air circulation. Paper cartons are o.k. to use for storage.)
4. Handle eggs as little as possible
   (except to turn them every few months for even drying, it is best not to tap them into each other for hairline cracks can occur.)
5. Keep the eggs from extreme heat or cold
   (Use no hot spotlights or storing in the attic where they may freeze in winter)
6. Do not take cold eggs from the refrigerator and submerge them in hot water to warm them for decorating. Allow them to come to room temperature normally.
7. If you live in a hot, humid climate, eggs should be blown for best results.

We have followed these rules and have been successful in preserving our eggs.

STAR

A geometric star, with eight points, is one of the oldest traditional Ukrainian designs. The varieties of interpretations of the star design can be enhanced by the imagination of the artist, as shown in the examples below.

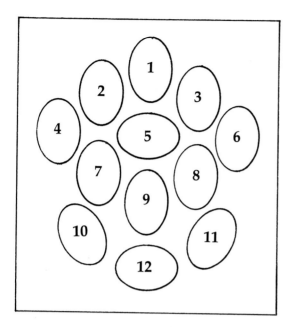

Color Combinations

The eggs shown on p. 95 have been made
by using the techniques described.
We have prepared the color sequences to
show you how the eggs were made.

Egg 1   dip into orange first,
dip into red
dip into black
bleach egg for final white
background

Egg 2   dip into brick brown dye
dip into black
bleach

Egg 3   work on white
dip into red
dip into orange
dip into green
dip into black

Egg 4   draw lines on white
dab green dots at center or flower
dip into orange
dip into green
soak green egg in water for lighter
background color

Egg 5   work on white
dip into yellow
dip into blue
then wash blue egg in water
dip into orange
dip into red for background

Egg 6   work on white
dip into yellow
dip into blue
dip into purple or royal blue
for final background

Egg 7   work on white
dip into light blue for
a longer period of time
to get a darker blue
work on blue
rinse in water for lighter
blue background

Egg 8   work on light brown
dip into brick brown
dip into orange for background

Egg 9   work on white
dip into yellow
dab orange
dab red
dip into light green
dip into blue
dip into black for background

Egg 10 dip first in red
dip into orange
dip into green
dip into black
bleach

Egg 11 dip into brick brown
dip into orange wash and then
into yellow
dip into green
dip into orange wash and then red
bleach

Egg 12 work on white
dip into yellow
dab on green
dip into orange
dip into red
dip into orange wash
then into green

Trypillian Background

The pottery and pysanky designs on page 98 and 99 are adapted from designs which came from an ancient tribe of people, Trypillians, who lived and thrived in the area of Ukraine 6,000 years ago. The society existed 3,000 years before biblical Abraham and long before Greek mythology and the bronze age. Trypillian people lived in the land of Ukraine at the same time as the Egyptian pyramids were built by the pharos and when Mesopotamia was born with its temples and kings.

At the end of the last century, an archeologist from Kiev found pieces of new kinds of pottery on the fields near the little city of Trypillia, 40 kilometers south of Kiev. Vikentiy Xvoika was looking for something else when he made the discovery of an ancient civilization. His work and studies centered around the Trypillian people and in his first published information in the historical magazine, *Kieve's Ancestry*, in 1899, he said, "This newly discovered culture belonged to the end of the Stone Age and the beginning of the Metal Age. On the pads of fired clay, a large number of whole and broken pieces of various forms were found. They were covered with original relief ornaments. Also, we found very interesting figures of people and animals, flint and polished rock tools. Works made from pure copper were unearthed. Some of the artifacts appear to be similar in appearance to works from Cyprus and Phonecia, and in general, one senses the influence of the East."

Studies of the culture have brought up historical information of interest in the construction of the villages. First, a large foundation was dug and leveled and a firm layer of fired clay bricks was placed at the bottom. Next, came a layer of wood and on top of this was one or two more layers of fired bricks. This was a floor which would last for centuries, also a floor which would handle moisture and be more comfortable because of its construction. The frames of the house were constructed of wood and then filled in with a wet clay mixture which contained sheaves of grasses to give it added strength. Houses were built in large square rectangles with round windows. It is believed that these structures were among the first square cornered buildings built up to this time.

The large houses were divided inside by two solid walls, creating three separate living units. Each area contained an oven, a sleeping area near the oven, and a stone mill for grinding the grains. Some scientists believed that the large buildings held three family units who were related to each other directly.

The rhythmical repeat patterns on the pottery and pysanky shown
here are adapted from the Trypillian artifacts found in Ukraine. The swirling
designs are believed to represent "mother earth" and the female, from whom
new life comes. The ceramics and the eggs were made by Luba Perchyshyn.

Village buildings were usually arranged in a loose large circular pattern with many structures scattered throughout the area. For many reasons, villages were located near rivers. The river brought wealth, food and convenience to the Trypillians. Because they settled widely, archeologists feel they could easily travel up and down stream and trade with other villages who were of the same tribe and spoke a common language.

One theory of the origin of the Trypillians tells us that they came from the area around the river Dunai, and brought grains and domestic animals with them to almost all areas of Ukraine. Like pioneers, they cleared the land and built their homes with only stone tools and settled in for a reign of highly developed and peaceful life. This was during the time the glaciers receded from the area of Ukraine, leaving a six-foot thick layer of rich top soil.

Evidence from the digs shows that the Trypillians were among the first tribes to plant grains and raise domestic animals such as cattle, sheep and pigs. Other tribes from the surrounding area had not developed these advanced ways and some evidence indicates that the Trypillians allowed other tribes to live with them. Archeologists believe the Trypillians taught others to build sturdier homes as opposed to their mud huts. They also taught them to make pottery far more useful and graceful than the crude pieces of the past.

Other great cultures of this time period and following periods used slavery as part of their structure. The Egyptians, Greeks, Romans and others built civilizations using labor of subjugated peoples. The Trypillians, however, were a matriarchal society that worshipped "mother earth" and had little interest in power struggles concerning politics, taxes, money and ruling, as in patriarchal societies.

Trypillians lived peacefully with each other and with their neighbors. The tools which were most used were hoes and sickles, not clubs and arrows. Their homes were decorated inside and out with beautiful drawings and paintings. Because they took time for artistic and aesthetic beauty, scientists feel they had enough food and time to spend on higher pursuits such as beauty and art.

Archeologists have divided the Trypillian society into three main periods, archaic (ascending), time of bloom (peak), and later (declining). More information is constantly being discovered, but many questions concerning the Trypillian culture remain to be answered. Among them are, why, in the many rich diggings, can no human bones be found? How did the Trypillians disappear? Why did scientists find their houses relatively intact, covered with earth, unbroken vases and statues still in their places? Were the Trypillians attacked by aggressive tribes? Did a plague strike and wipe out so many people that they could no longer survive? Many questions and hopefully many answers will come with future exploration and study. In the mean time, the Ukrainians of today are deeply interested in the Trypillians and are proud of the ancient people who once thrived on the steppes.

48 TRIANGLES

Another typical Ukrainian
design is the 48 TRIANGLES.
From the logical geometric
division of the egg, an infinity
of color combinations and
designs can be adapted, as
shown in the examples here.

SPIRALS

Many *pysanky* are divided into eight equal parts. A spiral design is added to this division for a basic design of elegant beauty. Some of the eggs below are so intricate that it is hard to recognize the original simple pattern.

Bibliography

Binyashevsky, Erast, compiled by, *Ukrainski Pysanky, Ukrainian Pysanky*, Kiev, Mystetstvo, Ukraine, 1968

Fasold, Hans, *Decorating Eggs*, Leisure Crafts, Search Press, London, England, 1968

Haupt-Battaglia, Heidi, *Oster Eier*, Published by Paul Haupt, Bern and Stuttgart, Switzerland, Germany, 1978

Humenna, Dokia, *The Past Is Flowing Into The Future*, Ukrainian Academy of Arts and Sciences in the United States, Inc., New York, 1978

Kylymnyk, Stephan, Professor, *Calendar Year in Ukrainian Folklore* Vol. III, Ukrainian Research Institute, Winnepeg, Toronto, Canada, 1962

Luciow, Johanna, Kmit, Ann, Luciow, Loretta, *Eggs Beautiful How to Make Ukrainian Easter Eggs*, Ukrainian Gift Shop, 2422 Central Avenue N.E., Minneapolis, Minnesota 55418, Harrison, Smith-Lund Press, Minneapolis, Minnesota, 1975

Markovich, Pavlo, *Pysanky, Naukoviv Zbirnyk* Vol. II, Viddili Ukrayinskoyi Literatury, Slovakia, 1972

Newall, Venetia, *An Egg at Easter*, Indiana University Press, Bloomington, Indiana, 1971

Newsome, Arden J., *Egg Craft*, Lothrop, Lee and Shepard Company, New York, 1973

Perchyshyn, Luba, *How to Decorate Beautiful Ukrainian Easter Eggs (Pysanky)*, Ukrainian Gift Shop, 2422 Central Avenue N.E., Minneapolis, Minnesota, 1976

Tkachuk, Mary, Kishchuk, Marie, Alice Nicholarchuk, *Pysanka: Icon of the Universe*, Ukrainian Museum, 910 Spadina Cresent East, Saskatoon, Sask., Canada, s7k 3g9, 1977

Index